Read & Understand
Grade 3
WITH LEVELED TEXTS

Writing: Jill Norris
Content Editing: Barbara Allman
De Gibbs
Copy Editing: Carrie Gwynne
Art Direction: Cheryl Puckett
Cover Design: Liliana Potigian
Illustration: Don Robison
Design/Production: Yuki Meyer
John D. Williams

EMC 3443

Visit
teaching-standards.com
to view a correlation
of this book.
This is a free service.

**Correlated to
Current Standards**

**Congratulations on your purchase of some of the
finest teaching materials in the world.**

*Photocopying the pages in this book
is permitted for <u>single-classroom use only</u>.
Making photocopies for additional classes
or schools is prohibited.*

For information about other Evan-Moor products, call 1-800-777-4362,
fax 1-800-777-4332, or visit our website, www.evan-moor.com.
Entire contents © 2010 Evan-Moor Corporation
18 Lower Ragsdale Drive, Monterey, CA 93940-5746. Printed in USA.

CPSIA: McNaughton & Gunn, Saline, MI USA [1/2022]

Contents

How to Use This Book

The Stories

The stories in this book include fairy tales, folk tales, realistic fiction, nonfiction, and poetry. With Lexile® scores ranging from 480 to 710, the reading levels span late second grade to beginning fourth grade.

Select a Story

Before selecting a story, determine how you will use the story.
Each story can be used

- as a directed lesson, with either an individual student or a group of students reading at the same level;
- by partners reading together; or
- for independent reading practice in the classroom or at home.

Preview the Story

1. Reproduce the story and give a copy to each student.
2. Discuss any vocabulary that might be difficult to decode or understand.
3. Have the students think about the title of the story and look at the picture or pictures to help them predict what the story is about.
4. Help students relate their prior knowledge and experience to the story.

Read the Story

A single story can be read for more than one purpose. You might first read the story for instructional purposes, and then have partners read the story again to improve comprehension and fluency. At a later time, you can use the story for independent reading. Each purpose calls for a different degree of story difficulty.

The Skill Pages

The five pages of reproducible activities that follow each story cover a variety of essential reading skills. The Skills Chart on page 5 provides an overview of the skills practiced in the activities. The focus skills for each activity are printed at the bottom of the worksheet. Each activity is suitable for either group instruction or independent practice.

Group Instruction

1. Reproduce the activity page for each student.
2. Make a transparency of the activity or write its content on the board.
3. Introduce the skill and guide students through the lesson.
4. Have students complete the activity as the group works through the lesson.

Independent Practice

Although many students will read the same story, they may each need to practice different skills. Assign the activities that are the most appropriate for each student's needs.

1. Be sure that the activity practices skills that have already been introduced to the student.
2. Review the directions and be sure that the student understands the task.
3. Go over the completed assignment with the student to assess his or her need for further practice.

Skills Chart

Stories	Letter/sound association	Categorizing/organizing	Predicting	Inferring/drawing conclusions	Syllabication	Synonyms/antonyms	Word endings	Contractions	Adjectives	Verbs/adverbs	Recalling information	Critical/creative thinking	Sequencing	Building vocabulary	Compare/contrast	Fact or fiction/opinion	Cause/effect	Problems/solutions	Relating personal information	Writing	Describing story characters
New Shoes	●			●		●		●	●		●	●		●					●	●	
The Wise Old Woman	●			●					●		●		●	●		●		●			●
The Messiest Room in Town	●		●	●			●				●			●					●		
A Grasshopper's Life Cycle	●			●						●	●		●	●		●					
The Three Sisters	●					●	●				●	●		●		●			●		●
The Dog Ate My Homework			●	●			●	●			●		●	●			●				
Off to California	●	●		●							●	●		●				●			
Harry's Helping Hand	●			●		●	●			●	●			●	●			●			
Hush, Little Baby	●	●	●	●			●	●			●	●		●	●				●	●	
The Fisherman and His Wife	●			●	●						●		●	●		●			●	●	
It's Not Fair!	●	●		●						●	●			●					●	●	
The Tortoise and the Hare	●			●	●						●	●	●	●							●
Let's Go Snorkeling	●	●		●			●				●	●	●	●							
Alligators and Crocodiles	●	●				●					●	●		●	●						
Daedalus and Icarus	●			●		●	●				●			●			●		●	●	
When Granny Met Johnny Appleseed	●			●		●					●	●		●						●	●
The Koala				●	●					●	●			●	●						
Shannon Lucid – Astronaut		●		●			●				●	●	●	●					●	●	
Vampire Bats	●			●	●						●	●		●	●	●			●	●	
George Washington Carver	●			●						●	●	●	●	●					●		●
Tornado!	●			●							●	●		●					●	●	

New Shoes

My shoes are new and squeaky shoes.
They're very shiny, creaky shoes.
I wish I had my leaky shoes
That Mother threw away.

I liked my old brown leaky shoes
Much better than these creaky shoes,
These shiny, creaky, squeaky shoes
I've got to wear today.

Read and Understand with Leveled Texts, Grade 3 • EMC 3443 • © Evan-Moor Corp.

Questions About *New Shoes* ·

1. What words are used to describe the new shoes?

   _____

2. What words are used to describe the old shoes?

   _____

3. Why do you think Mother threw away the old shoes?

   _____

4. Why do you think the boy wants his old shoes back?

   _____

5. Which words in the poem rhyme with **squeaky**?

   _____

Think About It ·

Design a machine to remove the "squeak" from new shoes.
Draw a picture of your machine and explain how it works.

_____

_____

Skills: Recall information to answer questions; draw conclusions; identify rhyming words; practice creative thinking.

What Does It Mean? ·····························

Match the words to the meanings.

shiny •   • letting water in

threw away •   • the contraction for **they are**

old •   • making a high, squealing sound

creaky •   • to put on

they're •   • bright and sparkling

wear •   • the contraction for **I have**

leaky •   • the opposite of **new**

wish •   • making a shrill, grating sound

I've •   • got rid of

squeaky •   • to want

On My Feet ······································

List types of shoes and other things you can wear on your feet.

1. _____

2. _____

3. _____

4. _____

5. _____

6. _____

Skills: Build vocabulary; recognize contractions; recognize opposites.

Read and Understand with Leveled Texts, Grade 3 • EMC 3443 • © Evan-Moor Corp.

Words Beginning with *thr* •

Fill in the letters **thr**. Then use the words to complete the sentences.

_____ew   _____ee   _____ush

_____oat   _____ead   _____eat

_____ough   _____ill   _____ob

1. Kim has a sore _____.

2. Sid _____ the ball to Marcus.

3. Mom used a needle and _____ to mend my shirt.

4. The bus went _____ a long tunnel.

5. My little brother is _____ years old.

6. A _____ was chirping in the apple tree.

The *eak* Word Family •

Use the clues to help you make words in the **eak** word family.

1. mountaintop   _____eak

2. to creep up   _____eak

3. a bird's bill   _____eak

4. not strong   _____eak

5. a noise a mouse makes   _____eak

6. to let water pass through   _____eak

7. to talk   _____eak

8. a noise an old door makes   _____eak

Skills: Make and use words with the initial blend **thr**; create a word family for **–eak**.   **9**

Homophones ·

Homophones are words that sound the same but are not spelled the same and have different meanings.

Write the correct homophone on each line.

byte   dough   rain
bear   flee   scent
bury   maize   through

1. bare _____   4. threw _____   7. bite _____

2. sent _____   5. berry _____   8. doe _____

3. flea _____   6. rein _____   9. maze _____

Using Homophones ·

Write the correct word to complete each sentence.

1. The _____ fell all day.
        rain   rein

2. The _____ was eating _____.
        bare   bear   buries   berries

3. Ted _____ the answer to the question.
        new   knew

4. Farmers _____ seeds in spring.
        sow   sew

5. Soo and Kim helped Mom make cookie _____.
                                dough   doe

6. Mark nailed a _____ on the fence to fix it.
        bored   board

7. She hurt her _____ when she stepped on a nail.
        he'll   heel

8. Angela _____ a letter to her friend.
        sent   scent

Skill: Identify and use homophones.

Read and Understand with Leveled Texts, Grade 3 • EMC 3443 • © Evan-Moor Corp.

Name _____

My Favorite Shoes ·

Draw your favorite pair of shoes.

1. Write four words that describe the shoes.

_____   _____

_____   _____

2. Why are they your favorite pair of shoes?

_____

_____

3. Write a two-line poem about the shoes.

_____

_____

Skills: Use adjectives; relate personal information to text; write a poem.   11

The Wise Old Woman

A wise old woman lived at the edge of the woods. Her son lived down the path and across the woods. One day, the old woman filled a basket with cookies for her son and started down the path into the woods. On the way, she met a bushy-tailed gray wolf. "I'm hungry," barked the wolf. "I'm going to eat you, old woman."

"Don't eat me now," said the old woman. "I'm just skin and bones. When I come back from my son's house, I will be fatter."

"Very well," said the wolf. "I will wait for you."

The old woman went on down the path. She saw a long green snake hanging from a tree. "I'm hungry," hissed the snake. "I'm going to eat you, old woman."

"Don't eat me now," said the old woman. "I'm just skin and bones. When I come back from my son's house, I will be fatter."

"Very well," said the snake. "I will wait for you."

The old woman went on down the path. She saw a big black bear crossing the path. "I'm hungry," growled the bear. "I'm going to eat you, old woman."

"Don't eat me now," said the old woman. "I'm just skin and bones. When I come back from my son's house, I will be fatter."

"Very well," said the bear. "I will wait for you."

Read and Understand with Leveled Texts, Grade 3 • EMC 3443 • © Evan-Moor Corp.

The wise old woman got to her son's house at lunchtime. They ate and ate. Then the old woman took a nap. After her nap, she said to her son, "Let's eat the cookies in the basket. Then I must go home."

When the cookies were gone, the old woman asked, "Son, may I have that giant pumpkin in your garden?"

The old woman cut open the giant pumpkin and took out all the seeds. She got into the pumpkin and rolled down the path into the woods. The bear saw the pumpkin roll by, but he was waiting for the old woman. The snake saw the pumpkin roll by, but he was waiting for the old woman, too.

After the pumpkin rolled past the wolf, it hit a big tree and broke open with a loud "crack!" The snake, the bear, and the wolf ran over to see what was going on.

"It's the old woman," barked the wolf. "I'm going to eat her!"

"No!" hissed the snake. "I'm going to eat her."

"No, no!" growled the bear. "I'm going to eat her."

The wise old woman looked at the animals and said, "The strongest of you can eat me."

While the animals were fighting over which was the strongest, the old woman ran away home.

Questions About *The Wise Old Woman* · · · · · · · · · · · · · ·

1. Where did the wise old woman live?

   _____

2. How did she get to her son's house?

   _____

3. Who did she meet on the way, and what did they want to do to her?

   _____

   _____

4. What did she do at her son's house?

   _____

5. Why did she want the giant pumpkin?

   _____

6. What are two wise things the old woman did? List them.

   _____

   _____

Think About It ·

How can you tell that this story is make-believe?

_____

_____

_____

Skills: Recall information to answer questions; draw conclusions; distinguish between real and make-believe.

Read and Understand with Leveled Texts, Grade 3 • EMC 3443 • © Evan-Moor Corp.

Name _____

What Does It Mean? ·

Match each word to what it means in the story.

old •   • not fat

wise •   • fell apart

giant •   • has lived a long time

path •   • along the outside

skin and bones •   • knows things

woods •   • needs food

broke •   • very big

edge •   • forests

hungry •   • a place to walk

Who Am I? ·

Who or what do the words describe? You may use a word more than once.

| bushy-tailed | green | gray | wise | big |
| skin and bones | hungry | long | black | old |

woman

_____

_____

_____

wolf

_____

_____

_____

snake

_____

_____

_____

bear

_____

_____

_____

The Sounds of *g* ·

Write **g** or **j** on each line to show the sound the letter **g** makes in the word.

1. got _____   5. edge _____

2. giant _____   6. goat _____

3. gum _____   7. gem _____

4. garden _____   8. girl _____

Write **g** or **j** on each line to complete the words.

_____um   _____am _____ar   _____iant

_____acks   _____orilla   _____eep

Who Owns It? ·

Write **'s** on the line to show who owns it.

1. son_____ pumpkin   4. pumpkin_____ seeds

2. old woman_____ basket   5. tree_____ branch

3. wolf_____ bushy tail   6. black bear_____ paw

Read and Understand with Leveled Texts, Grade 3 • EMC 3443 • © Evan-Moor Corp.

What Happened Next? ·

Cut and glue the sentences in order.

1. | glue |

2. | glue |

3. | glue |

4. | glue |

5. | glue |

6. | glue |

7. | glue |

The old woman got into the pumpkin and rolled into the woods.

The old woman filled a basket with cookies.

The pumpkin rolled past the bear, the snake, and the wolf.

The giant pumpkin hit a big tree and broke open.

"When I come back from my son's house, I will be fatter," she said.

The old woman ate and took a nap at her son's house.

While the animals were fighting, the old woman ran home.

Skill: Sequence story events.   17

Name _____

What Did the Old Woman Do? ·

Fill in the correct circle to tell how the wise old woman solved the problem.

1. The big bear wanted to eat her.
   Ⓐ She ran away.
   Ⓑ She told the bear to wait.
   Ⓒ She called for help.

2. The wise old woman had to go through the woods to get home.
   Ⓐ She went around the woods.
   Ⓑ She had her son go with her.
   Ⓒ She got into a pumpkin and rolled into the woods.

3. The pumpkin broke. The wolf, snake, and bear wanted to eat her.
   Ⓐ She got them to fight.
   Ⓑ She hit them with a big stick.
   Ⓒ She paid them to go away.

Draw the animals from the story.

bushy-tailed gray wolf

big black bear

long green snake
hanging from a tree

Skills: Identify problems and solutions; draw story characters.

The Messiest Room in Town

Everyone said Herbert's bedroom was the messiest room in town. It was littered with toys and clothes (clean and dirty). Pet hair, rotten apple cores, and moldy pizza scraps were all over the floor and under the bed. What a mess! But Herbert didn't care. He liked his room the way it was.

Herbert's mother said, "It smells in here! How do you stand it? And I'll bet you have dust bunnies under your bed."

"Not dust bunnies, dust monsters!" said his sister.

Herbert just grinned and closed the door. "Why do they care about my room?" he thought. "If I put things away, I won't be able to find them. Besides, I don't think it smells so bad in here."

One night, as Herbert was reading in bed, he heard a rumble. Then his bed began to move. When he looked up, he saw something coming out from under the bed.

Out popped two big brown eyes. Then out came a big brown nose with a clothespin stuck on the end. A dirty brown head came out next. It was a dust monster!

Read and Understand with Leveled Texts, Grade 3 • EMC 3443 • © Evan-Moor Corp.

The dust monster frowned. "Herbert," it said, "this room has passed messy. It has become a disaster area."

Herbert's only question was, "Why do you have a clothespin on your nose?"

"Because I can't stand the smell of dirty socks and rotten food," the monster answered. "It's time to clean up your mess."

The monster lurched over to a window and threw it open.

"Fresh air at last," the monster sighed.

Then the dust monster began to grow bigger and bigger.

"Clean up this room right now, Herbert!" it shouted. "If you don't, I will do something really terrible."

Herbert jumped out of bed. He quickly hung his clean clothes in the closet. He shoved his dirty clothes into a box by the door. He put his toys and books on shelves. As Herbert worked faster and faster, the dust monster got smaller and smaller. By the time Herbert was done, the monster was gone.

"Wow," said Herbert, "I'll never let my room get that messy again!" Then Herbert went to bed.

The next morning, everyone was shocked to see how neat and clean Herbert's room was. They wanted to know what had happened. Herbert just grinned as he put a "Keep Out" sign on the door.

Read and Understand with Leveled Texts, Grade 3 • EMC 3443 • © Evan-Moor Corp.

Questions About *The Messiest Room in Town* · · · · · · · · ·

1. What made people think Herbert had the messiest room in town?

   _____

2. Why did Herbert's room smell bad?

   _____

3. Why did the dust monster come out from under Herbert's bed?

   _____

4. Why did the dust monster have a clothespin on its nose?

   _____

5. What do you think the dust monster would have done
   if Herbert hadn't cleaned his room?

   _____

6. How did the bedroom get so messy?

   _____

Think About It ·

Circle the words that describe your bedroom.

   very messy   a little messy   neat and clean

How do you clean your room?

_____

_____

Skills: Recall information to answer questions; make predictions; make inferences; relate personal information to text.   **21**

Name _____

What Does It Mean? ·

Use the words in the word box to complete the puzzle.

Word Box

clothespin

core

disaster

dust

lurched

messiest

moldy

rotten

rumble

shocked

(puzzle grid with shaded column showing the letter **n**)

Clues

1. covered with a fuzzy growth
2. small bits of dirt
3. the biggest mess
4. a clip for hanging out clothes to dry
5. a noise
6. spoiled
7. very surprised
8. a bad happening
9. moved in a jerky way
10. the center of an apple

Use the words in the shaded boxes outlined in bold to complete this sentence.

A _____ is hiding under the bed!

Skill: Use story-related vocabulary to solve a puzzle.

Read and Understand with Leveled Texts, Grade 3 • EMC 3443 • © Evan-Moor Corp.

Short Vowel Sounds ·····························

Say each word below and write it under the letter that tells the short vowel sound you hear.

dollar	that	still	hush	in
get	rock	pup	sing	rest
can	bed	glass	tug	bottle
pocket	ring	tell	rattle	of

a	**e**	**i**	**o**	**u**
_____	_____	_____	_____	_____
_____	_____	_____	_____	_____
_____	_____	_____	_____	_____
_____	_____	_____	_____	_____

Add the Endings ·····························

Add **er** and **est** to each word. If the word ends in **y**, change the **y** to **i** before you add the ending.

	happy	happier	happiest
		er	**est**

1. small   _____   _____

2. messy   _____   _____

3. funny   _____   _____

4. silly   _____   _____

5. fast   _____   _____

6. tiny   _____   _____

Skills: Practice short vowel sounds; add the suffixes **er** and **est** to words ending in **y**.   23

Name _____

The Messy Bedroom ·

1. Circle the pillow on the floor.

2. Make an **X** on the pillow on the bed.

3. Color all the footwear brown.

4. Color the clothes red.

5. Draw an apple core and a half-eaten pizza on the floor.

6. How many toys do you see? _____

7. List four things that might be under the bed.

_____

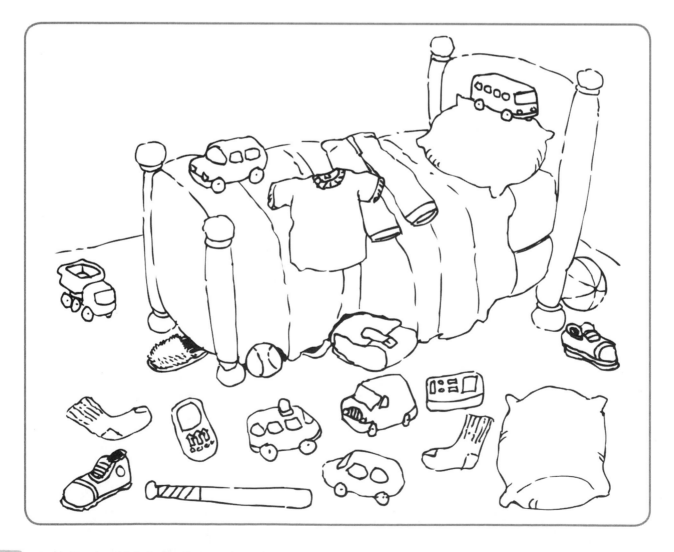

Skill: Read and follow directions.

Read and Understand with Leveled Texts, Grade 3 • EMC 3443 • © Evan-Moor Corp.

Read and Draw

Herbert was in bed, reading a book.	A dust monster came out from under the bed.
The dust monster threw open the window.	Herbert put a "Keep Out" sign on his bedroom door.

Skill: Draw to show comprehension of a sentence.   **25**

A Grasshopper's Life Cycle

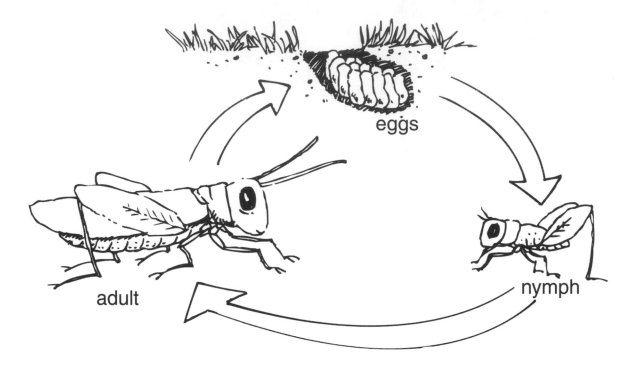

Grasshoppers lay their eggs in fall. The female grasshopper lays many eggs in a hole in the ground. The eggs stay in the ground for several months.

When spring comes, the new grasshoppers are born. Tiny grasshoppers called nymphs hatch from the eggs. The hungry little nymphs eat and grow. As they grow, they shed their skin many times. Shedding their skin is called molting.

At first, a grasshopper nymph has no wings. Its wings grow as the nymph grows and molts. With the last molt, the wings are fully grown. The nymph is now an adult grasshopper.

When fall comes, the female grasshoppers lay more eggs in the ground, and the cycle begins again.

Read and Understand with Leveled Texts, Grade 3 • EMC 3443 • © Evan-Moor Corp.

Questions About *A Grasshopper's Life Cycle* · · · · · · · · · ·

1. Where and when do female grasshoppers lay their eggs?

   _____

2. What are new grasshoppers called when they hatch?

   _____

3. Why does a grasshopper shed its skin?
   What is it called when this happens?

   _____

   _____

4. Name the following stages in a grasshopper's life cycle.

   _____   _____   _____

5. Why do you think this is called a life **cycle**?

   _____

   _____

Think About It ·

This story is about the life cycle of a grasshopper. Humans have a life cycle, too.
Think about what the stages of a human life cycle might be and write them below.

_____

_____

Skills: Recall information to answer questions; make inferences.

Name _____

What Happened Next? ·······················

Number the pictures in order. Write a sentence about what happens at each stage.

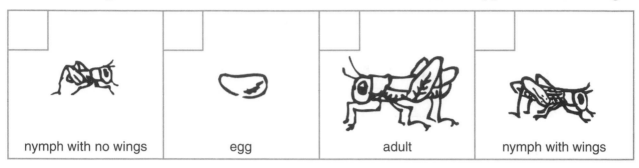

| nymph with no wings | egg | adult | nymph with wings |

1. _____

2. _____

3. _____

4. _____

The Parts of a Grasshopper ···················

Look at the parts of a moth. Read the labels.
A grasshopper has the same parts.
Label the parts below.

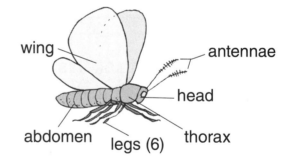

wing   antennae   head   abdomen   legs (6)   thorax

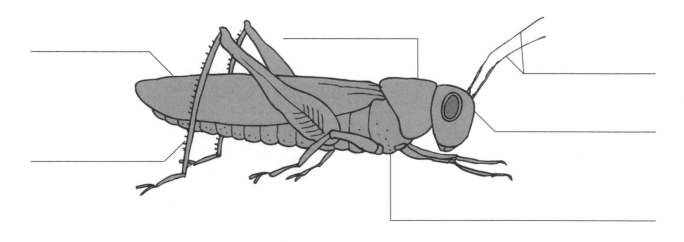

Skills: Sequence events in a life cycle; label a diagram.

Read and Understand with Leveled Texts, Grade 3 • EMC 3443 • © Evan-Moor Corp.

What Does It Mean? ·

Match each word to its meaning.

adult •   • the young of some insects

molt •   • to keep going

nymph •   • full-grown

female •   • to shed skin or feathers

several •   • the grasshopper that lays eggs

continue •   • more than two but not a lot

More Than One Meaning ·

Fill in the circle next to the correct meaning.

1. In the story, **hatch** means _____.
   Ⓐ a trapdoor covering
   Ⓑ to come out of an egg
   Ⓒ the opening in a ship's deck

2. In the story, **cycle** means _____.
   Ⓐ a long period of time
   Ⓑ to ride a bike or a motorcycle
   Ⓒ the stages in an insect's life

3. In the story, **shed** means _____.
   Ⓐ to throw off old skin
   Ⓑ a building used to store things
   Ⓒ to cry tears

Letters That Say /f/ ·······················

Circle the letters that make the **/f/** sound in each word.
Draw a picture to show what each word means.

finger	calf	telephone
nymph	coffee	alphabet

Past and Present ·························

Write the past tense of each word.

lays _____   come _____

eat _____   make _____

hatch _____   molt _____

grow _____   begin _____

send _____   sleeps _____

Use the past tense words you made to fill in the blanks.

1. Beth _____ me an e-mail message last night.

2. The female grasshopper _____ her eggs in fall.

3. The nymphs _____ several times as they _____.

4. We _____ all the pizza before Mom _____ home.

5. My baby sister _____ in the cradle Grandpa _____.

Read and Understand with Leveled Texts, Grade 3 • EMC 3443 • © Evan-Moor Corp.

Fact or Opinion? •

Make a check mark in the correct box to show if the statement
is a **fact** or an **opinion**.

	fact	opinion
1. Grasshoppers eat plants.		
2. Chocolate-covered grasshoppers taste good.		
3. Female grasshoppers lay eggs in the ground.		
4. A nymph is a young grasshopper.		
5. Grasshoppers are pretty insects.		
6. All grasshoppers should be killed.		
7. Grasshoppers have strong legs for hopping.		

Compound Words •

Circle the compound words in this paragraph. Write the words on the lines.

One morning, a cowgirl was riding across a field of sunflowers.
She was in a hurry to get back to the bunkhouse for breakfast. "I hope
we're having pancakes with peanut butter and applesauce," she said.
Just then, it started to rain. Her horse, Grasshopper, took off in a flash.
By the time they reached the ranch, the storm was over. A rainbow
was sparkling in the sunshine.

_____   _____   _____

_____   _____   _____

_____   _____   _____

The Three Sisters
A Native American Legend

Native Americans tell a story about three sisters who loved each other very much. Each one could be happy only when she was with her other two sisters.

The oldest sister stood tall and golden. She was graceful and strong. Her name was Corn.

The middle sister's name was Bean. She liked to twine around her sister Corn. As Bean grew taller, she could give Corn bigger and bigger hugs.

The youngest sister was very brave. She stayed at the feet of Corn and Bean to protect them from danger. Her name was Squash.

Where one of the sisters grew, the other two also wanted to grow. They never wanted to be apart. That's why they were always planted together in the same field.

On summer nights, when stars twinkled in the moonlit sky, the three sisters changed into young girls. Dressed in green, they danced and sang. They praised their Mother Earth and their Father Sun.

If you have a vegetable garden, think about planting corn, bean, and squash seeds in the same mound. Then you will have your own "three sisters" garden. Maybe some summer night, you'll see the three sisters dancing in the moonlight.

Read and Understand with Leveled Texts, Grade 3 • EMC 3443 • © Evan-Moor Corp.

Questions About *The Three Sisters* · · · · · · · · · · · · · · · · ·

1. What are the names of the three sisters?

   _____

2. What does Corn look like?

   _____

3. What does Bean do?

   _____

4. What is Squash's job?

   _____

5. What happens on moonlit nights?

   _____

6. What could be true in this story?

   _____

7. What parts of this story could <u>not</u> be true?

   _____

Think About It ·

A legend tries to explain things that happen in nature.
What does the legend of *The Three Sisters* tell us?

_____

_____

Skills: Recall information to answer questions; distinguish between real and make-believe; practice critical thinking.

Name _____

What Does It Mean? ·

Write each word next to its meaning.

mound   graceful   praise   twine

moonlit   Native Americans   protect   sisters

1. the first people to live in North America _____

2. girls with the same parents _____

3. moving in a smooth and easy way _____

4. to wind around _____

5. to keep safe _____

6. to worship in song _____

7. a hill of soil _____

8. lighted by the moon _____

Write the correct sister's name under each picture.

_____   _____   _____

Skills: Build vocabulary; use picture clues to identify story characters.

Read and Understand with Leveled Texts, Grade 3 • EMC 3443 • © Evan-Moor Corp.

Letters That Say Long e ·

Circle the letters that make the long **e** sound.

see	bean	weak
fleas	clean	three
seed	feet	please

Fill in the missing letters.

1. Did you s_____ the thr_____ sisters?

2. Are your hands cl_____n?

3. My dog has fl_____s.

4. Let's plant some b_____n s_____ds in the garden.

Add the Endings ·

Add **d** or **ed** to each word.

want_____   plant_____   love_____   stay_____

Write a sentence for each new word.

1. _____

2. _____

3. _____

4. _____

Skills: Identify letters that make the sound of long **e**; make and use words with **d** and **ed** suffixes.

Opposites ·

Match the opposites.

stay •   • youngest

oldest •   • hate

tall •   • go

love •   • winter

summer •   • day

father •   • short

night •   • mother

Same or Opposite? ·

Circle the pairs of words that have the same meaning.
Make an **X** on the pairs of words that have opposite meanings.

come – go   work – play

small – little   happy – jolly

below – under   dirty – clean

fat – thin   wet – dry

awake – asleep   sad – unhappy

late – early   scared – afraid

Name _____

Growing Vegetables ······································

Read and then answer the questions.

Do you have only a little space for a garden? Plant the "three sisters" together. The corn will grow tall and strong. The bean vine will climb up the cornstalk. The squash will grow around the bottom of the corn and bean plants. You can grow a lot of vegetables in a small space.

1. How can you plant corn, beans, and squash to fit in a small garden space?

   _____

   _____

2. List some of the vegetables that you have eaten.

   _____   _____

   _____   _____

   _____   _____

3. Draw the vegetables that you like best.

Skills: Read for information; relate personal information to text.   **37**

The Dog Ate My Homework

Kim woke up so happy this morning. It was Saturday, the sun was shining, and Kim was going to meet her friends at the park to play ball. After that, they were going to go to Jiffy Burger for lunch. Suddenly, Kim groaned, "Oh no! I can't go!" She had just remembered that she was on restriction. Here's why.

Tuesday: "Where's your homework, Kim?" asked Mr. Hobbs. "My dog ate it," Kim answered.

Wednesday: "Where's your homework, Kim?" asked Mr. Hobbs. "My baby brother ripped it up," Kim answered.

Thursday: "Where's your homework, Kim?" asked Mr. Hobbs. "It got washed down the kitchen drain," Kim answered.

Friday: "Where's your homework, Kim?" asked Mr. Hobbs. "I was too sick to do homework. I needed to rest," Kim answered.

That's when Mr. Hobbs called Kim's mother on the phone. The next thing Kim knew, her mom was at school, and Kim was in trouble—BIG trouble. She didn't even try to explain.

Now Kim is finishing last week's homework. And she's thinking about what she could have been doing instead on a sunny Saturday.

Read and Understand with Leveled Texts, Grade 3 • EMC 3443 • © Evan-Moor Corp.

Questions About *The Dog Ate My Homework* · · · · · · · · · · ·

1. Why was Kim on restriction?

   _____

2. What could Kim have been doing if she didn't have to finish last week's homework?

   _____

3. Which of Kim's excuses really could have happened?

   _____

   _____

4. Is there any way Kim's homework could have gone down the kitchen drain? Give a reason for your answer.

   _____

5. Would your teacher believe any of the excuses in this story? Give a reason for your answer.

   _____

Think About It ·

A **cause** is an event that makes something happen.
The thing that happens is the **effect**.

Fill in the missing cause and effect.

Cause: _____

Effect: The teacher called Kim's mother and asked her to come to the school.

Cause: Kim's mother went to the school and talked to the teacher.

Effect: _____

Read and Understand with Leveled Texts, Grade 3 • EMC 3443 • © Evan-Moor Corp.

Skills: Recall information to answer questions; draw conclusions; make predictions; identify cause and effect.

Name _____

What Does It Mean? ·

Write each word next to its meaning.

explain	drain	trouble
homework	groan	restriction

1. something that keeps you from
   doing something else   _____

2. a pipe that takes water out of a sink   _____

3. to give a reason for   _____

4. schoolwork that you do at home   _____

5. a problem   _____

6. an unhappy sound   _____

Contractions ·

Write the contractions.

1. I will   _____   4. that is   _____

2. did not   _____   5. could not   _____

3. will not   _____   6. where is   _____

The contractions below are often confused with the pronouns next to them.
Use the words correctly in the sentences to show what they mean.

they're – their	you're – your	it's – its

1. _____ going to _____ grandparent's house
   for Thanksgiving dinner.

2. _____ going to have to put _____ game away
   before you go to bed.

3. My dog knows _____ time for _____ bath.

Skills: Build vocabulary; make and use contractions.

Read and Understand with Leveled Texts, Grade 3 • EMC 3443 • © Evan-Moor Corp.

Name _____

Compound Words ···

Match the words to make compound words.

week •	• noon
sun •	• water
some •	• parents
after •	• end
home •	• thing
under •	• book
apple •	• work
grand •	• shine
skate •	• sauce
note •	• board

Draw a picture of the compound word in each box.

spaceship	grasshopper
watermelon	peanut

Skills: Make compound words; draw pictures to build vocabulary.   41

Name _____

Add the Endings ·

less means *without*   **ful** means *full of*
er means *a person who*   **ly** tells *in what manner*

Add the ending that makes the correct word.

1. without harm   harm_____

2. a person who teaches   teach_____

3. full of joy   joy_____

4. in a sad way   sad_____

5. without a home   home_____

6. full of care   care_____

7. a person who sings   sing_____

8. in a quick way   quick_____

Base Words and Endings · · · · · · · · · · · · · · · ·

Write the base word on the first line. Write the ending
on the second line.

1. restless   _____   _____

2. slowly   _____   _____

3. player   _____   _____

4. nicely   _____   _____

5. wonderful   _____   _____

6. careless   _____   _____

7. dreamer   _____   _____

Skills: Add suffixes; identify base words and suffixes.

Read and Understand with Leveled Texts, Grade 3 • EMC 3443 • © Evan-Moor Corp.

What Happened Next? ·

Pretend that you are Kim. Write a letter to a friend.
Tell your friend how you got into trouble, in the order it happened.

Dear _____,

_____

_____

_____

_____

_____

_____

_____

_____

_____

_____

_____

Your friend,
Kim

Skill: Sequence story events.   **43**

Off to California

"Laura," Mama called. "It's time to go."

Mama and Papa were just about finished packing up the car. Papa was tying a mattress to the roof of the car. Mama was putting her pots and pans among the clothes and tools in the trunk. It was time to load the children and the dog into the back seat and hit the road. Papa wanted to get an early start. It would take four or five days to get to California.

Mama looked around and muttered, "Where is that child? I told her we'd be leaving right after breakfast."

Laura was hiding in the barn. She was huddled in a corner, clinging to a wiggling kitten.

"I won't go, Skeeter," she sobbed. "I won't go without you. Who will take care of you if I go? It's not fair to leave you behind. Dog gets to go. Why can't you go, too? I won't go if you can't go. I just won't!"

Mama looked for Laura in the treehouse and under the porch. As she walked past the barn, she heard Laura crying. Mama went in and sat down beside her weeping daughter.

Read and Understand with Leveled Texts, Grade 3 • EMC 3443 • © Evan-Moor Corp.

"I know you're unhappy," said Mama, giving Laura a hug. "But we have to go. Times are hard. There's no work here for Papa. Uncle Henry says he can help Papa find work if we come to his place in California."

Laura petted her kitten as she listened to Mama talk.

"You know, Laura, we all have to leave behind things we love," Mama continued. "We had to sell your sister's piano and your brother's horse. And Papa and I can't take much from the house. It's hard on everyone. We just don't have a choice right now. Papa has to have work."

Laura looked up at Mama and whispered, "Will we ever get to come back home?"

Mama smiled and wiped away Laura's tears. "We're going to make a new home in California," she explained. "When times are better, we'll come back for a good long visit. I know it doesn't seem fair that Dog gets to go and Skeeter can't. We're taking Dog because he's a good watchdog. Skeeter can't do much to help, but don't worry about her. Aunt Lizzie will take good care of Skeeter. She has always wanted a kitten."

Laura got up and hugged Mama. "I'll go find Aunt Lizzie," she said. She was determined now to be brave and helpful as the family set off to California.

Read and Understand with Leveled Texts, Grade 3 • EMC 3443 • © Evan-Moor Corp.

Questions About *Off to California* ·

1. Why was Laura's family moving to California?

   _____

2. What did Mama and Papa pack in the trunk for the trip?

   _____

3. Why was Laura hiding in the barn?

   _____

4. Mama was upset with Laura at the beginning of the story.
   Why was she so kind to Laura when she found her in the barn?

   _____

   _____

5. What did Mama say that made Laura feel better?

   _____

   _____

6. Why do you think Mama and Papa sold the piano and the horse
   instead of leaving them with someone?

   _____

Think About It ·

Think about how you would feel if your family had to move far away with only
what would fit in the car. List three reasons you would be unhappy.

_____

_____

_____

Skills: Recall information to answer questions; draw conclusions; make inferences; practice critical thinking.

Read and Understand with Leveled Texts, Grade 3 • EMC 3443 • © Evan-Moor Corp.

What Does It Mean? ··

Write each word next to its meaning.

cling   determined   mutter

choice   huddle   porch

1. to complain or grumble   _____

2. to crowd close together   _____

3. to hold on tight to something   _____

4. a covered entrance to a building   _____

5. the power to choose   _____

6. having your mind firmly made up   _____

More Than One Meaning ·····································

Fill in the circle next to the correct meaning.

1. In the word **watchdog**, what does **watch** mean?
   Ⓐ to keep guard
   Ⓑ a device for telling time
   Ⓒ to look at something for some purpose

2. How is the word **fair** used in the story?
   Ⓐ a place to show farm produce and animals
   Ⓑ giving the same treatment to all
   Ⓒ having light-colored skin

3. What kind of **trunk** is being filled in the story?
   Ⓐ an elephant's long nose
   Ⓑ a tree's main stem
   Ⓒ a car's storage compartment

Name _____

Word Webs •

Write each word in a box on the correct word web.

aunt	explained	trunk	Skeeter
back seat	Laura	roof	whispered
brother	cried	sister	
Lizzie	muttered	parents	

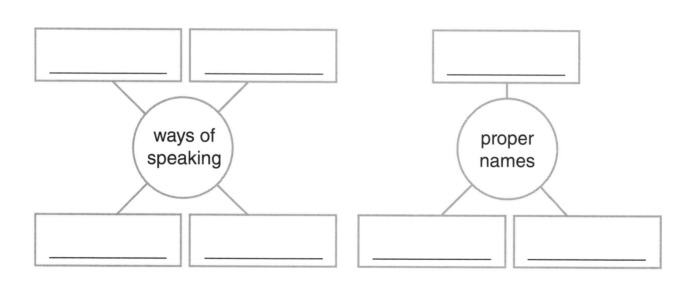

ways of speaking

proper names

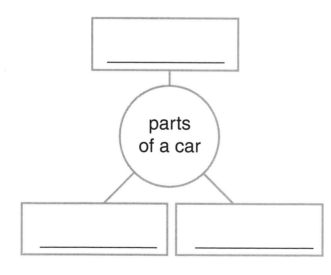

parts of a car

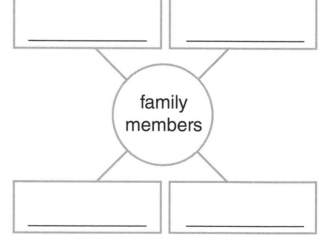

family members

Skills: Categorize words; use a graphic organizer (word web).

Read and Understand with Leveled Texts, Grade 3 • EMC 3443 • © Evan-Moor Corp.

Where Do You Hear Long *o*? •

Circle the words that have the long **o** sound.

open	out	foam	come	doctor
hello	often	of	whole	piano
flower	throat	joke	load	owner
stone	know	mower	now	gone

Write each of the long **o** words you circled in the correct category.

o–e	**open syllable**	**oa**	**ow**
_____	_____	_____	_____
_____	_____	_____	_____
_____	_____	_____	_____

The Sounds of *ed* •

Write each word under the sound that **ed** makes in the word.

cooked	headed	planned	hunted
traveled	washed	wanted	picked
played	begged	baked	planted

ed	**d**	**t**
_____	_____	_____
_____	_____	_____
_____	_____	_____
_____	_____	_____

Name _____

Dear Diary,

This has been a crazy day. We had just started down the road this morning when we heard "thump-thump, thump-thump." It was a flat tire! We didn't have a spare tire. Papa had to walk almost two miles before he found a place to get the tire fixed. And he had to use up all of our gas money to pay for fixing it.

Papa and Mama were worried about the gas money. Then a farmer came by in his truck. He asked if we'd like to pick corn for him. Papa, Mama, and Sis picked corn all afternoon. They made enough money for gas and food for about two days. Papa says that will get us to Uncle Henry's place in California.

While they were gone picking corn, Dog took off after a rabbit. I wanted to go find him, but my brother said we couldn't leave the car and all our stuff to go after him. He said that a dog will come back on its own when it gets hungry. That's all for now.

Good news! A man just came by to see if we had lost a dog. It sure is good to have Dog back.

Find three problems in the story above. Write the problems and solutions.

Problem: _____

Solution: _____

Problem: _____

Solution: _____

Problem: _____

Solution: _____

Read and Understand with Leveled Texts, Grade 3 • EMC 3443 • © Evan-Moor Corp.

Harry's Helping Hand

Hi! I'm Harry. I have to be in a wheelchair all day. The muscles in my arms and legs are weak. I can't use my legs at all, and I'm not too great with my hands either. When I drop something, it stays dropped until someone picks it up for me. I can't open doors or turn lights on and off. Carrying the things I need for school is a problem, too. Life has been kind of difficult for me.

But now things are easier. I have a helping hand—or, I should say, a helping paw. I have Pete! Pete is a golden retriever that has been trained to help kids like me. He went to service-dog school for two years to learn how to do dozens of different tasks. I had to be trained, too. I had to learn how to give Pete commands and how to take care of him.

When Pete is working, he doesn't play around. My friends know that they are not to pet or call Pete when he's working. Pete pulls my wheelchair and picks up things I drop. He carries my school books and my lunch in his backpack. He pushes the button on the school elevator and opens some kinds of doors. He even knows how to turn on lights.

Pete is here when I need a helping hand. But best of all, Pete is here when I need a friend.

Questions About *Harry's Helping Hand* ·················

1. Why does Harry need help?

   _____

2. How does Pete help Harry?

   _____

3. Where did Pete learn his skills?

   _____

4. Why did Harry need training?

   _____

5. Why can't people pet Pete when he's working?

   _____

6. Who would these dogs help?

   seeing service dogs: _____

   hearing service dogs: _____

Think About It ·····································

Fill in the blanks with information from the story.

Characters: _____   _____

Problem: _____

_____

Solution: _____

_____

Skills: Recall information to answer questions; draw conclusions; make inferences; identify problems and solutions.

Read and Understand with Leveled Texts, Grade 3 • EMC 3443 • © Evan-Moor Corp.

What Does It Mean? ·

Use these words to complete the paragraph below.

wheelchairs	problems	tasks
service dogs	taught	trained

Dogs must be _____ to help disabled people.

The dogs go to school for a long time to be _____.

They must learn how to do many different _____ before

they are ready to be helpful. Some _____ help people

who have to be in _____ all day. The dogs can help

solve _____ for their human partners.

Comparing Things ·

Write the word that completes each comparison.

1. **hand** is to **person** as **paw** is to _____

2. **ear** is to **hear** as **eye** is to _____

3. **moon** is to **night** as **sun** is to _____

4. **bird** is to **fly** as **fish** is to _____

5. **cookie** is to **eat** as **milk** is to _____

6. **giant** is to **large** as **elf** is to _____

7. **on** is to **off** as **in** is to _____

8. **chair** is to **sit on** as **bed** is to _____

Skills: Build vocabulary; complete analogies to make comparisons.

Present Tense Verbs ·

Add **s** or **es** to each verb.

stay _____   know _____   drop _____

push _____   open _____   take _____

pick _____   use _____   wash _____

Use the new words to complete the sentences.

1. Pete _____ with Harry all day and all night.

2. Harry _____ good care of Pete.

3. Pete _____ the door for Harry.

4. Pete _____ how to turn on the lights.

5. Pete _____ his dish with his nose when he wants dinner.

6. Harry _____ colored markers to draw pictures.

7. Harry _____ Pete in the shower.

8. Pete _____ up things that Harry _____.

Add the Ending ·

Change the **y** to **i** and add **es**.

1. carry _____   5. worry _____

2. fly _____   6. study _____

3. hurry _____   7. try _____

4. cry _____   8. bury _____

Skills: Use present tense verbs; add the suffix **es** to words that end in **y**.

Read and Understand with Leveled Texts, Grade 3 • EMC 3443 • © Evan-Moor Corp.

The Sounds of *oo* ·

Write each word under the correct sound.

look	loose	good	soon
smooth	goose	hook	stood
balloon	shampoo	cookie	brook

boo**k**   sch**oo**l

_____ _____   _____ _____

_____ _____   _____ _____

_____ _____   _____ _____

Opposites ·

Circle the words that are opposites in each sentence.

1. Tanisha closed the door Lee had opened.

2. We have to do our work before we can play.

3. Maria says math is easy, but science is difficult.

4. Do you know the answer to that question?

5. Lee pulled the wagon while Carlos and Sam pushed it.

6. I want to learn to play checkers so I can teach my friends.

7. The truck went under the bridge before it went over the mountain.

8. Cary was so excited, he was laughing and crying at the same time.

Opposites Crossword Puzzle ·

Write the opposite of the clue to solve the puzzle.
Use the words in the word box.

Word Box

- end
- enemy
- few
- go
- here
- lower
- noisy
- question
- quiet
- same
- something
- together
- wrong

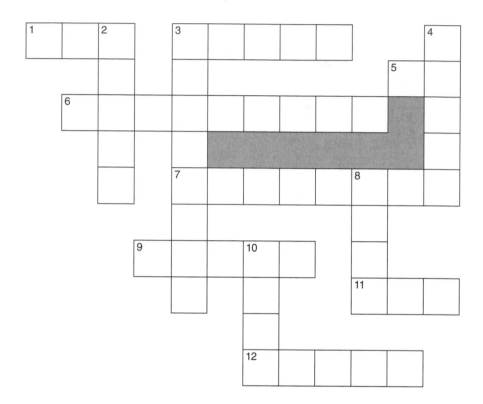

Across
1. many
3. noisy
5. stay
6. nothing
7. apart
9. quiet
11. begin
12. friend

Down
2. right
3. answer
4. higher
8. there
10. different

Skills: Identify antonyms to solve a crossword puzzle.

Read and Understand with Leveled Texts, Grade 3 • EMC 3443 • © Evan-Moor Corp.

Hush, Little Baby
A Lullaby

Hush, little baby, don't say a word.
Papa's going to buy you a mockingbird.

If that mockingbird won't sing,
Papa's going to buy you a diamond ring.

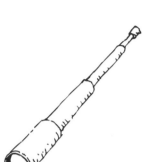

If that diamond ring turns brass,
Papa's going to buy you a looking glass.

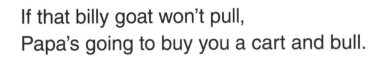

If that looking glass gets broke,
Papa's going to buy you a billy goat.

If that billy goat won't pull,
Papa's going to buy you a cart and bull.

If that cart and bull turn over,
Papa's going to buy you a dog named Rover.

If the dog named Rover won't bark,
Papa's going to buy you a horse and cart.

If that horse and cart fall down,
You'll still be the sweetest little baby in town.

Questions About *Hush, Little Baby* · · · · · · · · · · · · · · · · · ·

1. Who is singing to the baby in the lullaby?

   _____

2. Why do people sing lullabies to babies?

   _____

3. List the things Papa says he will buy.

   _____   _____

   _____   _____

   _____   _____

   _____   _____

4. What might go wrong with the following gifts?

   diamond ring   _____

   looking glass   _____

   cart and bull   _____

   Rover the dog   _____

5. What words describe the baby? _____

Think About It ·

Papa sang about some unusual baby gifts.
Write what you think a baby would really like to have.

_____

_____

_____

Skills: Recall information to answer questions; draw conclusions; make predictions; practice critical thinking.

Read and Understand with Leveled Texts, Grade 3 • EMC 3443 • © Evan-Moor Corp.

Name _____

Rhyming Words •

Find the word in the lullaby that rhymes with each of the following words.
Then write another word that rhymes with each pair.

1. word _____ _____

2. glass _____ _____

3. sing _____ _____

4. down _____ _____

5. pull _____ _____

Circle the rhyming pairs. Make an **X** on pairs that do <u>not</u> rhyme.

brass – glass	fell – bell	broke – goat
over – cover	bark – cart	buy – fly
you – shoe	come – home	papa – saw

Contractions •

Write the long form of each contraction.
Write the numbered letters in the boxes at the bottom to name a fun snack.

don't _____ _____ _____ _____ _____
                                2

you'll _____ _____ _____ _____ _____ _____ _____ _____

won't _____ _____ _____ _____ _____ _____
                                        5

Papa's _____ _____ _____ _____ _____ _____
           1   3

can't _____ _____ _____ _____ _____
           4

isn't _____ _____ _____ _____ _____
                        7

they're _____ _____ _____ _____ _____ _____ _____
                                        6

1	2	3	4	5	6	7

Skills: Identify and make rhyming words; understand contractions. **59**

Letters That Say Long *i* ·

i–e	ie	y
mine	lie	fly

Write the long **i** word that names each picture.

Comparing Things ·

Use **er** to compare two things. Use **est** to compare many things.

Write **er** or **est** on each line.

1. Hummingbirds are the small_____ birds.

   A robin is small_____ than an eagle.

2. Jay runs fast_____ than Pete.

   He is the fast_____ runner in class.

3. My brother is tall_____ than me.

   My dad is the tall_____ person in our family.

Skills: Identify letters that make the sound of long i; use the suffixes **er** and **est** to make comparisons.

Read and Understand with Leveled Texts, Grade 3 • EMC 3443 • © Evan-Moor Corp.

What Does It Mean? •

Find the words in the song that go with the meanings below.
Write the words on the lines next to their meanings.

  1. a piece of jewelry   _____

  2. a sweet-singing bird   _____

  3. a male goat   _____

  4. to pay money for   _____

  5. a two-wheeled vehicle   _____

  6. a small telescope   _____

What's My Name? •

Write each name on the line below the correct picture.

    billy goat   mockingbird   baby

    horse and cart   diamond ring   looking glass

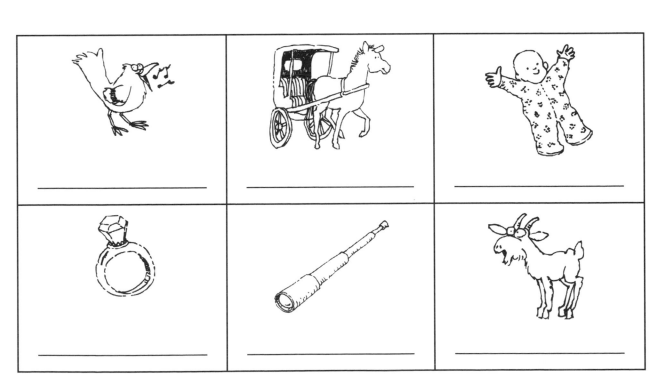

Good Night, Sleep Tight ·

Hush, Little Baby is a lullaby. Lullabies are sung to babies and young children to help them go to sleep.

Write about how your parents got you to go to sleep when you were a baby.

_____

_____

_____

_____

_____

My Favorite Lullaby ·

Ask ten classmates to name their favorite lullaby. Complete this list.

classmate asked	favorite lullaby
1. _____	_____
2. _____	_____
3. _____	_____
4. _____	_____
5. _____	_____
6. _____	_____
7. _____	_____
8. _____	_____
9. _____	_____
10. _____	_____

Skills: Write a personal narrative; organize information on a list.

Read and Understand with Leveled Texts, Grade 3 • EMC 3443 • © Evan-Moor Corp.

The Fisherman and His Wife

Once upon a time, long, long ago, there lived a fisherman and his wife. They were very poor. They lived in an old wooden hut by the seashore. All they had to eat were fish that the husband caught and vegetables that the wife grew in her garden. The husband was content going to fish in the sea each day, but his wife wanted more.

One day, the fisherman caught an unusual fish. As he looked at the fish, it began to speak.

"I am an enchanted prince," said the fish. "Please put me back into the water before I die." The kindhearted fisherman put the fish back into the water and went home.

"I caught a talking fish today," he told his wife. "It was really an enchanted prince." The fisherman's wife became very excited.

"Go back and call the fish," she demanded. "You saved its life. It should give you a reward. Tell it you want a cottage."

The fisherman went back to the seashore and called, "Magic fish, I am the fisherman who put you back into the water. May I talk to you?"

Read and Understand with Leveled Texts, Grade 3 • EMC 3443 • © Evan-Moor Corp.

When the fish appeared, the fisherman asked for a cottage.

"Go home," said the fish. "It is done."

When the fisherman got home, he saw a new cottage standing in place of the old wooden hut. His wife was happy for a while, but then she wanted more.

One day she said, "I am uncomfortable in this small cottage. Go back and tell the fish I want a castle. I want to be a queen."

The fisherman went to the seashore and called for the magic fish. He told the fish that his wife wanted to be a queen and live in a castle.

"Go home," said the fish. "It is done."

When the fisherman got home, he saw the castle. His wife was happy for a while, but then she wanted more. She wanted to rule the world. She sent her husband to the seashore again.

When the fish appeared, the fisherman explained that, now, his wife was unhappy being a queen. She wanted to rule the world.

"Go home," said the fish. "It is done."

The greedy wife was happy for a while, but then she started to think about how she had no control over day and night. Once more, she sent her husband to talk to the fish.

When the fisherman told the magic fish that his wife wanted to rule the sun and the moon, the fish became angry.

"You ask for too much!" the fish shouted. "Go home!"

When the fisherman got home, all he saw was the old wooden hut. Once again, his greedy wife grows vegetables in her garden. And the contented fisherman goes to the sea to catch fish for supper.

Read and Understand with Leveled Texts, Grade 3 • EMC 3443 • © Evan-Moor Corp.

Questions About *The Fisherman and His Wife* · · · · · · · · ·

1. What did the fisherman do each day?

   _____

2. What was unusual about the fish he caught?

   _____

3. Why did his wife keep sending the fisherman back to see the fish?

   _____

4. Why did the fish agree to grant the wife's wishes?

   _____

5. What made the fish angry? How did it show that it was angry?

   _____

6. What word is used to describe the fisherman's wife?

   _____

7. What do you think the moral (lesson) of the story is?

   _____

Think About It ·

What would you ask for if you caught an enchanted fish? Why?

_____

_____

_____

_____

Skills: Recall information to answer questions; draw conclusions; write a personal narrative. **65**

What Happened Next? •

Write the sentences in the order that they happened in the story.

His wife wanted to rule the world.

The fisherman caught an enchanted fish.

His wife sent him to ask for a castle.

The angry fish shouted, "You ask for too much!"

Once upon a time, there lived a poor fisherman and his wife.

His wife sent him to ask for a cottage.

The couple were back in their old hut.

His wife wanted to control day and night.

1. _____

2. _____

3. _____

4. _____

5. _____

6. _____

7. _____

8. _____

Read and Understand with Leveled Texts, Grade 3 • EMC 3443 • © Evan-Moor Corp.

What Does It Mean? ·

Match each word to what it means in the story.

supper •

unusual •

enchanted •

contented •

greedy •

couple •

appear •

explain •

rule •

• wanting more than your share

• satisfied

• to come into sight

• under a magic spell

• to make the meaning clear

• an evening meal

• to have control over

• strange or rare

• two people who are married to each other

Draw a picture to show the meaning of each word.

cottage	castle

Skill: Build vocabulary. **67**

The Sounds of c •

Write the letter **s** or **k** on the line to show the sound
that **c** makes in the word.

cent _____   candy _____

once _____   magic _____

cereal _____   city _____

canary _____   popcorn _____

fence _____   pancake _____

cut _____   pencil _____

Un Means *not* •

Add **un** to each word. Then use each new word in a sentence.

_____usual   _____comfortable   _____happy

1. _____

   _____

2. _____

   _____

3. _____

   _____

Skills: Practice the sounds of hard and soft **c**; make and use words with the prefix **un**.

Read and Understand with Leveled Texts, Grade 3 • EMC 3443 • © Evan-Moor Corp.

How Many Syllables? •

Find words in the story that have two, three, and four syllables.
List the words under the correct headings.

2 syllables	3 syllables	4 syllables
_____	_____	_____
_____	_____	_____
_____	_____	
_____	_____	
_____	_____	

Write a sentence that contains both of the four-syllable words.

_____

_____

Real and Make-Believe •

List three things in the story that could really happen.

1. _____

2. _____

3. _____

List three ways you can tell that this story is make-believe.

1. _____

2. _____

3. _____

Skills: Count syllables; distinguish between real and make-believe.   **69**

It's Not Fair!

Being the middle kid stinks! I'm always too young or too old for things. Mom and Dad don't listen when I say it's not fair. I made a couple of lists to show them how bad it is being in the middle.

Here is my list of complaints about my big sister.

1. She gets to stay up late watching television.
2. She goes to her friends' houses on school nights.
3. She gets to go places, like the mall, without an adult.
4. She gets a really big allowance.
5. She gets to shop for her own clothes without Mom or Dad going along.
6. She has her own computer in her bedroom.

When I ask for these things, my parents just say, "You're too young for that yet."

Read and Understand with Leveled Texts, Grade 3 • EMC 3443 • © Evan-Moor Corp.

Then, there's my little brother.

1. He gets to sleep as late as he wants to every morning.

2. He gets to eat yummy mashed potatoes, while I have to eat lima beans.

3. Someone reads to him before his nap and before he goes to sleep at night.

4. He has some great toys that I never get to use.

5. We always have the baby sitter he likes when Mom and Dad go out.

6. He can make a big mess, and no one complains or makes him clean it up.

When I ask for these things, my parents just say, "You're too old for that anymore."

Being the middle kid stinks! It's not fair!

Questions About *It's Not Fair!* ·

1. What was the boy in the story complaining about?

   _____

   _____

2. What are three things his parents said he was too young for?

   a. _____

   b. _____

   c. _____

3. What are three things his parents said he was too old for?

   a. _____

   b. _____

   c. _____

Think About It ·

How old do you think the boy's big sister is? Why?

_____

_____

How old do you think the boy's little brother is? Why?

_____

_____

Read and Understand with Leveled Texts, Grade 3 • EMC 3443 • © Evan-Moor Corp.

What Does It Mean? ·

Fill in the circle next to each correct answer.

1. What does **stinks** mean in the story?
   - Ⓐ smells bad
   - Ⓑ is not fair
   - Ⓒ moves slowly

2. What can you do at a **mall**?
   - Ⓐ shop for things
   - Ⓑ plant flowers
   - Ⓒ find something to eat

3. What does **allowance** mean in the story?
   - Ⓐ permission to do something
   - Ⓑ the brim on a hat
   - Ⓒ money a parent gives a child

4. What are you doing when you **complain**?
   - Ⓐ telling what you want
   - Ⓑ saying you don't like something
   - Ⓒ writing a thank-you note

5. Which word is the opposite of **young**?
   - Ⓐ child
   - Ⓑ old
   - Ⓒ new

6. Which of these people is an **adult**?
   - Ⓐ your mother
   - Ⓑ your father
   - Ⓒ a grown-up

Write sentences to show that you know what these words mean.

fair _____

baby sitter _____

lima beans _____

Skill: Build vocabulary. **73**

Silent Letters ·

Say each word. Cross out the letter or letters that do <u>not</u> make a sound.

listen	write	knit
talk	climb	sign

Use the past tense form of the words to fill in the blanks.

1. I _____ a letter and _____ my name at the end.

2. Carlos _____ to the top of the tree.

3. Tanisha _____ a sweater for her baby sister.

4. We _____ to what the teacher said, and then

   we _____ about it.

Word Families ·

Read the clues to make words in the **ight** and **old** word families.

to argue with someone	_____ight
not dark	_____ight
the opposite of **day**	_____ight
the sense we use to see	_____ight
too snug	_____ight
brave	_____old
the opposite of **hot**	_____old
to bend in half	_____old
spoke to someone	_____old
it grows on old food	_____old

Read and Understand with Leveled Texts, Grade 3 • EMC 3443 • © Evan-Moor Corp.

Skills: Identify silent letters; make and use past tense verbs; create word families for **–ight** and **–old**.

Can You Do It? ●

Cut and glue the phrases to show which ones someone your age can do and which ones you are too young for.

I can do it.	I am too young.
glue	glue

drive a car	work in an office
fly a kite	fix my own breakfast
stay out until midnight	go to R-rated movies
stay overnight with a friend	use in-line skates
play soccer	rent an apartment

Skills: Draw conclusions; categorize information.   **75**

It's Not Fair! ·

What would you like to do that your parents think you are too old for?
Why do you think that you are young enough?

_____

_____

_____

_____

_____

What would you like to do that your parents think you are too young for?
Why do you think that you are old enough?

_____

_____

_____

_____

_____

Read and Understand with Leveled Texts, Grade 3 • EMC 3443 • © Evan-Moor Corp.

The Tortoise and the Hare

One fine summer day, Hare was showing off to the other animals. "I'm faster than any animal in the woods," Hare boasted. "None of you is as quick as I am."

Slow-moving Tortoise was passing by and heard what Hare was saying. "I know someone who can beat you in a race," said Tortoise. "Me!"

Hare nearly fell down laughing at the thought of such a poky animal beating him in a race. "Very well," said Hare. "I will race you, and I will win!"

The other animals marked off a racecourse through the woods. Tortoise and Hare came to the starting line.

"Get ready. Get set. Go!" shouted Owl.

Hare raced off as fast as he could go. Soon, he was so far ahead that he could not see slow-moving Tortoise.

Read and Understand with Leveled Texts, Grade 3 • EMC 3443 • © Evan-Moor Corp.

"I think I'll take a little nap under this shady tree," Hare decided. "Tortoise is so far behind, he will never catch up." Soon, Hare was fast asleep.

Slowly and steadily, Tortoise moved along the racecourse. He quietly passed the sleeping Hare and continued on his way. When Hare woke up from his nap, he didn't see Tortoise anywhere.

"I knew that silly tortoise was the slowest animal on earth," Hare laughed as he continued the race. Suddenly, Hare heard some loud shouting. "What is that?" he wondered.

Hurrying toward the sounds, he saw that Tortoise was only a few feet from the finish line. The loud shouting he had heard was the sound of the other animals cheering for Tortoise.

Hare raced as fast as he could, but there was no way he could get to the finish line before Tortoise did. While the other animals congratulated Tortoise, the embarrassed Hare quietly crept away.

The moral of this story is: Slow and steady wins the race.

Read and Understand with Leveled Texts, Grade 3 • EMC 3443 • © Evan-Moor Corp.

Questions About *The Tortoise and the Hare* · · · · · · · · · ·

1. What part did Owl play in the race between Tortoise and Hare?

   _____

2. Why did the speedy Hare lose the race?

   _____

3. Circle the words that describe Tortoise.
   Make an **X** on the words that describe Hare.

quick	poky	unkind
steady	embarrassed	well-liked
foolish	slow-moving	showoff

4. What is the moral of the story?

   _____

   _____

Think About It ·

Why do you think Hare always bragged about his speed to the other animals?

_____

_____

_____

_____

What Does It Mean? ·

Find the word in the story that goes with each meaning.
Write the word on the line next to the meaning.

1. a kind of turtle   _____

2. praised for winning   _____

3. uneasy and ashamed   _____

4. sneaked   _____

5. an animal like a rabbit   _____

6. with a regular motion   _____

7. bragged   _____

Antonyms ·

Antonyms are words that mean the opposite.

         Hare was **fast**.   Tortoise was **slow**.

Write the correct antonym for the underlined word in each sentence.

sunny	quickly	winter	lost
cried	loudly	behind	finish

1. It was a fine <u>summer</u> day.   _____

2. Tortoise moved <u>slowly</u>.   _____

3. Hare <u>laughed</u> at the poky tortoise.   _____

4. Owl said "Go!" to <u>start</u> the race.   _____

5. Hare was far <u>ahead</u> of Tortoise.   _____

6. He stopped under a <u>shady</u> tree.   _____

7. Tortoise <u>quietly</u> passed Hare.   _____

8. Tortoise <u>won</u> the race.   _____

Skills: Build vocabulary; identify antonyms.

Read and Understand with Leveled Texts, Grade 3 • EMC 3443 • © Evan-Moor Corp.

Letters that Say Long o

o	o–e	oa	oe	ew	ow
piano	rope	road	toe	sew	follow

Write the long **o** word that names each picture.

The Sounds of *gh*

The letters **gh** can sound like the letter **f**. They can also be silent.

Say each word. Circle **f** or **silent** to tell what sound you hear **gh** make.

laugh	f	silent		thought	f	silent
tough	f	silent		daughter	f	silent
night	f	silent		eight	f	silent
cough	f	silent		enough	f	silent

Skills: Use letter combinations that make the sound of long **o**; practice the /f/ sound of **gh** and silent **gh**.   **81**

Name _____

Adverbs ·

An adverb that ends in **ly** usually tells how something is done.

Fill in the missing adverb in each sentence.

> happily   steadily   slowly   angrily

1. A tortoise moves _____ most of the time.

2. They worked _____ all day to finish the job.

3. The animals cheered _____ when Tortoise won the race.

4. The boy shouted _____ when the dog took his sandwich.

Add **ly** to the words below to make adverbs. If the word ends in **y**, change the **y** to **i** before you add **ly**.

> steady + ly = stead**i**ly   happy + ly = happ**i**ly

1. sleepy _____   4. handy _____

2. sudden _____   5. quick _____

3. loud _____   6. pretty _____

Write sentences using at least three of the adverbs you made.

1. _____

_____

2. _____

_____

3. _____

_____

Skill: Make and use adverbs that end in **ly**.

An Interview •

A reporter from the local television station is interviewing Hare and Tortoise at the scene of the big race. Write the answers that you think Hare and Tortoise would give to the reporter.

Before the race:

Reporter: Why are you racing Tortoise today?

Hare: _____

Reporter: How easy do you think it will be to win the race?

Hare: _____

Reporter: Tortoise, why do you think you can beat Hare?

Tortoise: _____

Reporter: What is your plan for beating Hare in the race?

Tortoise: _____

After the race:

Reporter: Congratulations, Tortoise! At what point did you
know you would win the race?

Tortoise: _____

Reporter: I can't talk to Hare about the race. He seems
to have disappeared.

Let's Go Snorkeling

My Aunt Gertie likes to try new things. Not only does she want to try them, she wants you to try them, too. When you see her with a big grin on her face, you know something is about to happen. The next thing you know, Aunt Gertie is saying, "Let's have an adventure."

Our last adventure together was a trip to the Hawaiian Islands. Aunt Gertie wanted to go snorkeling to see the beautiful ocean fish and underwater plants. But the adventure didn't start when we got on the airplane. We had a lot to learn before we headed to the islands.

We took snorkeling classes at the sports center. We had to learn how to breathe with a snorkel and how to dive and swim wearing a mask and fins. We also learned safety tips.

Next, we went to buy our equipment. We each got a snorkel, which is a tube that is used for breathing. One end goes in your mouth. The other end sticks out of the water. And we each bought a face mask to keep water out of our eyes and nose. We also bought fins to wear on our feet. Fins help you have more power when you kick your feet as you swim.

At last we were ready to go. We packed our clothes and equipment and went to the airport. As soon as we landed, we checked in at the hotel. Then we changed into our swimsuits and headed for the beach. Aunt Gertie couldn't wait another minute to start our underwater adventure.

Uh-oh! Aunt Gertie is starting to grin again. What will her next adventure be?

Questions About *Let's Go Snorkeling* · · · · · · · · · · · · · · · ·

1. What makes Aunt Gertie's nephew think she's so interesting?

   _____

2. What might you see when you go snorkeling?

   _____

   _____

3. What equipment do you need for snorkeling? Tell how each is used.

   a. _____

   b. _____

   c. _____

4. Why is it important to be trained before you go snorkeling?

   _____

   _____

Think About It ·

Circle **yes** or **no**.

Would you like to go snorkeling?   yes   no

Give three reasons for your answer.

1. _____

2. _____

3. _____

Skills: Recall information to answer questions; make inferences; draw conclusions; practice critical thinking.

Name _____

What Does It Mean? •••••••••••••••••••••••••••••••••

Put these words from the story into the correct categories.

airport	fins	kick
breathe	sports center	hotel
face mask	Hawaiian Islands	swim
dive	snorkel	swimsuit

places	**what you wear when you're snorkeling**	**actions**
_____	_____	_____
_____	_____	_____
_____	_____	_____
_____	_____	_____

Label each piece of equipment.

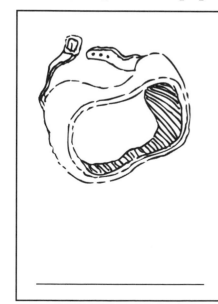

_____

_____

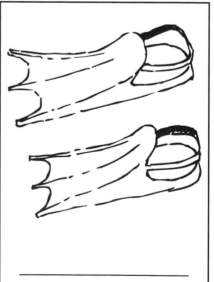

_____

Skills: List theme-related vocabulary words in categories; use picture clues to practice vocabulary.

Read and Understand with Leveled Texts, Grade 3 • EMC 3443 • © Evan-Moor Corp.

Letters That Say Long *i* ·

i	i–e	igh	uy	y
climb	dive	high	buy	dry
islands	line	sight	guy	fly

Fill in the missing long **i** words in this paragraph.

I took lessons to learn how to _____ into the water

wearing a snorkel. After each lesson, I _____ out of

the pool and _____ off with my towel. When I completed

all the lessons, Aunt Gertie took me to _____ snorkeling

equipment. The cost of some items was very _____.

Tomorrow, we're going to get on a plane and _____ to

the Hawaiian _____ for a snorkeling holiday.

More Than One ·

Write the plural form of each word. Use **s** or **es** for most words.
Change **y** at the end to **i** and add **es**. Some of the words have special plurals.

1. fin _____

2. class _____

3. berry _____

4. man _____

5. book _____

6. dish _____

7. baby _____

8. island _____

9. beach _____

10. woman _____

11. bunny _____

12. jet _____

13. child _____

14. house _____

15. goose _____

16. story _____

Skills: Use letter combinations that make the sound of long **i**; add the suffixes **s** and **es** to make plurals.

What Happened Next? ·

Cut out the sentences and glue them in the order they happened.

1. | glue |

2. | glue |

3. | glue |

4. | glue |

5. | glue |

6. | glue |

We took classes to learn how to use the equipment.

Aunt Gertie said, "Let's have an adventure."

We changed into our swimsuits and headed for the beach.

Aunt Gertie and I flew to the Hawaiian Islands.

We bought snorkels, face masks, and fins.

Aunt Gertie is grinning again. What will her next adventure be?

Read and Understand with Leveled Texts, Grade 3 • EMC 3443 • © Evan-Moor Corp.

Find the Answers ·····················

You want to learn how to snorkel. Read the sign and follow the directions.

1. Draw a red circle around the words that tell how much the lessons cost.

2. Draw a blue box around the words that tell where you have to go for the lessons.

3. Draw a green line under the day that the lessons are given. Draw two green lines under the time.

4. Are you old enough to take the lessons?   yes   no

Learn to Snorkel

Markham Sports Center
Saturday, 8:00–10:00 a.m.
6 lessons: $50
Must be 8 years or older.

Snorkeling Word Search ·····················

```
a d v e n t u r e x e s
h v w s n o r k e l q a
a i r p o r t i m i u f
w g o o s w i m p s i e
a f t r d i v e l l p t
i f i t s a w e a a m y
i z u s m a s k b n e n
f i n s h f l y t d n w
u n d e r w a t e r t e
l p a r n q h o t e l t
```

Find each word in the puzzle and circle it. Then check off the word on the list.

_____ adventure	_____ fins	_____ island	_____ sports
_____ airport	_____ fish	_____ mask	_____ swim
_____ dive	_____ Hawaii	_____ safety	_____ trip
_____ equipment	_____ hotel	_____ snorkel	_____ underwater

Skills: Read and follow directions; use visual discrimination to find story-related vocabulary in a word search puzzle.

Alligators and Crocodiles

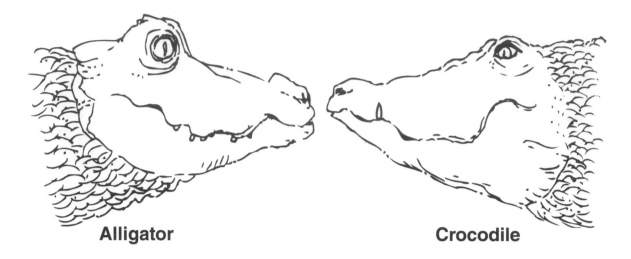

Alligator   **Crocodile**

Alligators and crocodiles are reptiles. Like all reptiles, they have dry, scaly skin and lay eggs. They are coldblooded. This means they can't make heat to keep their bodies warm. They have to be in a warm place to stay warm. That's why most alligators and crocodiles live in hot climates.

These reptiles are good swimmers. They swim by moving their long, strong tails. Most kinds of alligators and crocodiles live near fresh water. A few kinds live near rivers that flow into the sea. The water is salty there.

Their bodies are well-suited to life in the water. With their eyes and nostrils on top of their heads, they can see and breathe when their bodies are in the water. A transparent flap of skin protects each eye. Their nostrils close to keep water out.

An alligator has a wide, round snout. A crocodile's snout is narrower. One bottom tooth shows on each side of a crocodile's closed mouth, but not on an alligator's.

Alligators and crocodiles are hunters. Lying still in the water, their greenish-brown bodies look like big logs. This often tricks other animals into coming close—and becoming dinner! Alligators and crocodiles eat large animals, such as cattle. They also eat small animals like birds and fish. They use their powerful tails, sharp teeth, and strong jaws to catch food.

Read and Understand with Leveled Texts, Grade 3 • EMC 3443 • © Evan-Moor Corp.

Their teeth are not good for tearing or chewing. They shake their prey to break off big chunks. Then they swallow the chunks whole. They often lose teeth, but new ones grow in quickly. They might grow fifty or more sets of teeth in a lifetime.

On land, an alligator slithers along on its stomach with its legs spread out to the sides. A crocodile moves quickly, using its front and back legs together.

A mother crocodile digs a nest in the sand for her eggs. She lays the eggs and then covers them up. A mother alligator lays her eggs in a pile of rotting plants and mud. When the eggs are ready to hatch, the babies make noises in their shells. Then the mothers uncover the nests.

In the nest, the hatchlings eat small worms, snails, and insects. As soon as they leave the nest, they head for water. Most alligators and some crocodiles help their babies get to the water. They carry the babies in their mouths or on their backs. The mothers look after their young while the babies are small. Still, many young alligators and crocodiles are eaten by other animals before they grow up.

Questions About *Alligators and Crocodiles* · · · · · · · · · · · ·

1. Describe a reptile.

   _____

   _____

2. Why do reptiles need to live where it's warm?

   _____

   _____

3. List three ways alligators and crocodiles are suited for life in the water.

   a. _____

   b. _____

   c. _____

4. What is unusual about the teeth of alligators and crocodiles?

   _____

5. How do alligators and crocodiles know when their eggs are ready to hatch?

   _____

Think About It ·

Why is it a bad idea to sell baby alligators and crocodiles as pets?

_____

_____

_____

_____

Skills: Recall information to answer questions; practice critical thinking.

Read and Understand with Leveled Texts, Grade 3 • EMC 3443 • © Evan-Moor Corp.

What Does It Mean? ·

Fill in the circle next to each correct answer.

1. Which word tells what is on the outside of a **reptile**?
   Ⓐ fur
   Ⓑ scales
   Ⓒ feathers

2. What does **prey** mean in the story?
   Ⓐ animals that are caught for food
   Ⓑ to say grace
   Ⓒ scaly animals

3. What is the **climate** of a place?
   Ⓐ how high it is there
   Ⓑ how the weather is there
   Ⓒ how many people live there

4. Which animals are **reptiles**?
   Ⓐ snake
   Ⓑ alligator
   Ⓒ turtle

5. Which words mean the opposite of **fresh water**?
   Ⓐ muddy water
   Ⓑ new water
   Ⓒ salty water

Use clues in the story to help you write the meaning of these words.

1. coldblooded _____

2. hatchling _____

3. transparent _____

Skills: Build vocabulary; use context clues to define words. **93**

Letters That Say *er* ··

Circle the letters that say **er** in each of these words.

water   bird   turn   word   earn

Use the letters you circled to fill in the missing letters in the words below.

My moth_____ is a n_____se. H_____ w_____k is very

important. Last Friday aft_____noon, she left w_____k _____ly

so we could go to the movies togeth_____. But f_____st, we ate

at the pizza parl_____ next to the movie theat_____.

The movie was about a gigantic monst_____ that was

cov_____ed with f_____. The monst_____ went around frightening

everyone on _____th.

Articles ··

The articles **a** and **an** come before nouns.
Use **a** before nouns that start with a consonant.
Use **an** before nouns that start with a vowel.

Write **a** or **an** on each line.

_____ alligator	_____ crocodile	_____ egg
_____ nest	_____ octopus	_____ pony
_____ angel	_____ snout	_____ orange
_____ tail	_____ insect	_____ tooth

Read and Understand with Leveled Texts, Grade 3 • EMC 3443 • © Evan-Moor Corp.

Antonyms ·

Write each word on the line next to the word that means the opposite.

asleep	full	light	slow
clean	happy	night	small
cooked	hard	safe	warm

1. soft _____

2. angry _____

3. huge _____

4. rapid _____

5. day _____

6. dangerous _____

7. chilly _____

8. empty _____

9. heavy _____

10. awake _____

11. raw _____

12. dirty _____

What Doesn't Belong? ·

Cross out the word in each group that does not belong.

eyes mouth toes nostrils	alligator turtle snake bird	pond river creek stream
capture release trap catch	hat bonnet cap ribbon	chair bench table stool

Alligator and Crocodile ·

Fill in the chart to show the differences between an alligator and a crocodile.

	Alligator	Crocodile
how it moves on land		
shape of snout		
position of teeth		
nest material and location		

Skills: Complete a chart to compare and contrast.

Read and Understand with Leveled Texts, Grade 3 • EMC 3443 • © Evan-Moor Corp.

Daedalus and Icarus
A Greek Myth

Pronunciation Key	
Daedalus	**ded** • l • uhs
Minos	**my** • nuhs
Icarus	**ik** • uh • ruhs
Sicily	**sis** • uh • lee

Daedalus was an architect and an inventor. King Minos hired Daedalus to design his palace. Minos was the king of the island of Crete. King Minos became angry with Daedalus when he helped one of the king's enemies escape. The king made Daedalus and his son, Icarus, his prisoners. He would not let them leave Crete.

Daedalus told his son, "There is no escape by land, and Minos controls the sea. But he does not control the air. That is how we will escape!"

Icarus gathered feathers of the gulls that soared over the island. Daedalus designed a pair of wings. He made a wooden frame and attached gull feathers to it with wax and string. Then he studied the flight of the island birds. Daedalus learned how they moved their wings. He also watched how the birds hovered on air currents. When the wings were ready, Daedalus called Icarus to him.

"My son," he said, "what we are about to do is very dangerous. Listen carefully to what I say. Keep to the middle path between heaven and earth. Do not go too near the sun. Its heat will melt the wax. Do not go too near the sea. The fog will wet the feathers, and the wings will become too heavy. Stay close to me, and no harm will come to you."

At first, Icarus followed his father as he had been told. But soon, he wanted to fly higher. Up, up, up, he flew, ignoring his father's warning cry.

When he felt warm wax running over his shoulders, Icarus realized his mistake. He tried to flutter his wings, but no feathers remained. Icarus fell from the sky! He plunged into the sea and drowned.

Daedalus hurried to save his son, but he was too late. He picked up Icarus and flew to land. After Daedalus buried Icarus, he flew to the island of Sicily. He remained in Sicily for the rest of his life.

Read and Understand with Leveled Texts, Grade 3 • EMC 3443 • © Evan-Moor Corp.

Questions About *Daedalus and Icarus* · · · · · · · · · · · · · · · · · ·

1. Why did Daedalus and Icarus have to escape by air?

   _____

2. What were their wings made of?

   _____

3. Why did Daedalus watch flying birds?

   _____

4. Why did Icarus's wings fall apart?

   _____

5. Why should Icarus have listened to his father's instructions?

   _____

6. What two islands are named in the story?

   _____

Think About It ·

Think of a time when you did <u>not</u> listen to a warning or an instruction.
Tell what happened.

_____

_____

_____

_____

Skills: Recall information to answer questions; make inferences; write a personal narrative. **99**

What Does It Mean? ·

Match each word to its meaning.

inventor •　　　　　　　　• to fall

soar •　　　　　　　　• to move through the air

design •　　　　　　　　• a creator of new things

hover •　　　　　　　　• injury or damage

warning •　　　　　　　　• to make a plan

ignore •　　　　　　　　• to not pay attention to

plunge •　　　　　　　　• to remain in one place in the air

harm •　　　　　　　　• a notice of danger

To – Too – Two ·

The words **to**, **too**, and **two** are homophones.
They have different spellings, but they all sound the same.

Fill in the blanks with the correct homophone.

1. Juan planned a trip _____ the aquarium.

2. Alan needs _____ new tires for his bike.

3. Kelly wants new tires, _____.

Write a sentence using each homophone.

to _____

too _____

two _____

Read and Understand with Leveled Texts, Grade 3 • EMC 3443 • © Evan-Moor Corp.

The Sounds of *ou* ·

Listen to the sound of **ou** in each word. Write the symbol
for the sound on the line next to the word.

ow	loud	$\breve{oo}$	could	$\bar{o}$	though
aw	thought	$\bar{oo}$	tour	$\breve{u}$	country

1. should _____   9. about _____

2. shoulder _____   10. couple _____

3. cloud _____   11. ouch _____

4. cousin _____   12. cough _____

5. you _____   13. would _____

6. bought _____   14. court _____

7. hour _____   15. your _____

8. boulder _____   16. enough _____

Synonyms ·

Match the words that mean about the same thing.

design •   • collect

angry •   • caution

gather •   • injury

dangerous •   • mad

middle •   • plan

near •   • fall

harm •   • center

warn •   • close

remain •   • unsafe

plunge •   • stay

Skills: Practice the sounds of **ou**; recognize synonyms.

Name _____

Add the Endings ··

Write each base word with the suffixes to make new words.

1. Drop the **e** and add the endings **ing** and **ed**.

   move   _____   _____

   hope   _____   _____

   smile   _____   _____

   Just add **s** at the end.

   move   _____

   hope   _____

   smile   _____

2. Double the last letter and add the endings **ed** and **ing**.

   hop   _____   _____

   control _____   _____

   plan   _____   _____

   Just add **s** at the end.

   hop   _____

   control _____

   plan   _____

3. Change **y** to **i** and add the endings **es** and **ed**.

   hurry   _____   _____

   study   _____   _____

   bury   _____   _____

   Just add **ing** at the end.

   hurry   _____

   study   _____

   bury   _____

Read and Understand with Leveled Texts, Grade 3 • EMC 3443 • © Evan-Moor Corp.

Cause and Effect ·

Write the effect of each cause listed below.

Cause	Effect
The king was angry and would not let Daedalus leave the island.	_____ _____
The king controlled the land and the sea.	_____ _____
Icarus ignored his father's warning about flying too near the sun.	_____ _____

Draw What Happened ·

Daedalus built a pair of wings.	Icarus flew too near the sun.

Skills: Determine cause and effect; illustrate story events. **103**

When Granny Met Johnny Appleseed

"Tell us a story, Granny," begged the children.

Granny was the best storyteller in the whole state. She was very, very old and had lived in many places. She had experienced many adventures and knew many interesting people.

"Well, you youngins have been mighty good all day," said Granny. "I guess I can remember one story. Did I ever tell you about the time I met Johnny Appleseed?"

"You met Johnny Appleseed?" asked the children.

"Yep," answered Granny.

"I was just a little mite when Ma, Pa, and me headed west. It was a long, hard trip, travelin' by covered wagon. When we stopped, Pa would collect firewood, and Ma would start supper. While Pa took care of the oxen and Ma cooked, I was supposed to stay out of the way.

"Well, one evening, while I was stayin' out of the way, I spied a little rabbit. It was as cute as a button. I set out followin' that rabbit, and the next thing I knew, I was lost in the woods. I started to blubber, and tears ran down my cheeks. Then I started to bawl big, loud sobs.

" 'My, my, what's the matter youngin'?' asked a funny-looking old man. 'Why are you raisin' such a ruckus? Are you lost?'

Read and Understand with Leveled Texts, Grade 3 • EMC 3443 • © Evan-Moor Corp.

"I whispered, 'Yes.'

"He said, 'Now don't you be scared. I'll take you back to your folks.'

"I'd never seen anyone that looked so strange. He was dressed in worn-out old clothes, his feet were bare, and he had on a funny hat. But I wasn't afraid. He had a kind smile and a twinkle in his eyes.

" 'Folks call me Johnny Appleseed,' he said after Ma and Pa thanked him for finding me.

"Ma invited Johnny to eat with us. While we ate, he told us how he was travelin' west with his apple seeds. Everywhere he stopped, he planted apple seeds and made friends. He was friendly with Indians, settlers, and the wild animals in the woods.

"After supper, Johnny gave me a handful of apple seeds. 'Plant these seeds when you settle, youngin',' he said. Then he disappeared into the woods."

"Did you plant the seeds, Granny?" asked the children.

"Yep," said Granny. "Look out the window. You can see them growin' on the side of the hill. And I've got me a hankerin' right now to pick some and make an apple pie for supper."

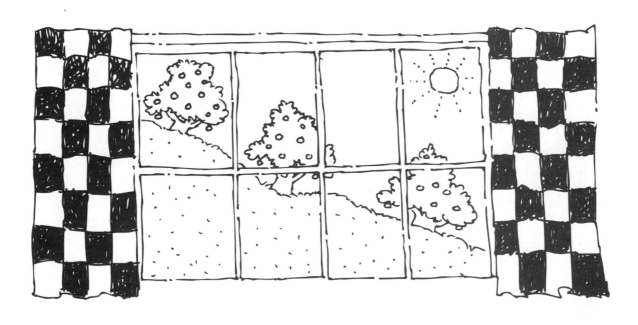

Questions About *When Granny Met Johnny Appleseed*

1. Why did Granny agree to tell the children a story?

   _____

2. Where was Granny's family headed in their covered wagon?

   _____

3. How did Granny get lost in the woods?

   _____

4. Describe the man who found Granny in the woods.

   _____

5. Why wasn't Granny afraid of the man?

   _____

6. How did Johnny Appleseed get his nickname?

   _____

7. Where did the apple trees on the hill at Granny's house come from?

   _____

8. Granny planned to make an apple pie for supper.
   What is another way she could have used the apples?

   _____

Think About It •

Do you think it's possible that Granny really met Johnny Appleseed?
Tell why or why not.

_____

_____

_____

Skills: Recall information to answer questions; make inferences; draw conclusions; practice critical thinking.

Read and Understand with Leveled Texts, Grade 3 • EMC 3443 • © Evan-Moor Corp.

Name _____

Add *ing* •

In the story, the letter **g** was dropped from many words with an **ing** ending and was replaced with an apostrophe. In the past, many people spoke that way. Some people still do. Write the correct spelling of the underlined words in these sentences.

1. We were <u>travelin'</u> west in a covered wagon.   _____

2. I was <u>stayin'</u> out of the way while Ma cooked.   _____

3. The bear cub was <u>followin'</u> its mother.   _____

4. Granny is <u>raisin'</u> apples on the hillside.   _____

5. She was <u>wishin'</u> for a pet of her very own.   _____

6. They were <u>goin'</u> for a walk in the park.   _____

Similes •

A simile compares things in an interesting or funny way, using the words **like** or **as**.

The rabbit was **as cute as a button**.

Match the parts of the following similes.

as mad •   • as a mule
as stubborn •   • as an owl
as wise •   • as a penny
as strong •   • as a bug in a rug
as bright •   • as a wet hen
as snug •   • as an ox

Write your own similes.

1. as big as _____

2. as cold as _____

3. as fast as _____

4. as old as _____

Skills: Interpret colloquial word endings; recognize and use similes.   **107**

Name _____

What Does It Mean? ·

Fill in the circle next to the correct answer.

1. **Youngins** are _____.
   Ⓐ children
   Ⓑ old men
   Ⓒ apple seeds

2. When you **blubber**, you are _____.
   Ⓐ making bubbles
   Ⓑ taking a bath
   Ⓒ crying

3. If you answer **yep**, you are saying _____.
   Ⓐ no
   Ⓑ yes
   Ⓒ maybe

4. A **ruckus** is a _____.
   Ⓐ broken toy
   Ⓑ noisy commotion
   Ⓒ kind of backpack

5. If you have a **hankerin'**, you _____.
   Ⓐ want to do or to have something
   Ⓑ need a handkerchief
   Ⓒ have a headache

6. In the story, the word **folks** is used to mean _____.
   Ⓐ Granny and the children
   Ⓑ Ma and Pa
   Ⓒ people Johnny met

7. In the story, **mighty** means _____.
   Ⓐ strong
   Ⓑ big
   Ⓒ very

Skill: Define colloquial language.

Read and Understand with Leveled Texts, Grade 3 • EMC 3443 • © Evan-Moor Corp.

Spelling the Long *a* Sound ···

Circle the correct spelling.

1. _____ your hand if you have a question.   raise   rase

2. Mother set the flowers on the _____.   table   tayble

3. Mario is the best _____ in our league.   plaier   player

4. My grandparents flew here on a jet _____.   plane   plain

5. Don't be _____ to try new things.   afrade   afraid

6. The astronaut flew into outer _____.   spayce   space

7. Kelly broke the white _____ in her box.   crayon   craone

8. Mr. Lee was elected _____ of the city.   maire   mayor

Pronouns ··

I	we	it	he	she	they
me	us	you	him	her	them

Replace each underlined noun with the correct pronoun.

1. <u>Granny</u> is a great storyteller.   _____

2. Ma invited <u>Johnny</u> to eat supper.   _____

3. I followed <u>the rabbit</u> into the woods.   _____

4. <u>Ma and Pa</u> worked hard.   _____

5. Granny picked <u>apples</u> for a pie.   _____

6. <u>Johnny</u> planted apple seeds.   _____

7. Granny made pie for <u>Ma and me</u>.   _____

8. <u>Ma and I</u> like apple pie.   _____

Skills: Spell words with letter combinations that make the sound of long **a**; replace nouns with pronouns.

Name _____

Who Was Johnny Appleseed? ·

Find out more about the real man who was called Johnny Appleseed.
Write a paragraph about what you learned.

I read: _____
(title of book, magazine, or encyclopedia)

This is what I learned:

_____

_____

_____

_____

_____

_____

_____

_____

_____

_____

_____

Draw Johnny Appleseed.

Skills: Read to find information; write and draw to record information.

Read and Understand with Leveled Texts, Grade 3 • EMC 3443 • © Evan-Moor Corp.

The Koala

The koala is a mammal that lives in Australia. In many ways, it is like any other mammal. It has thick fur. Its young are born live. The young drink milk from the mother's body.

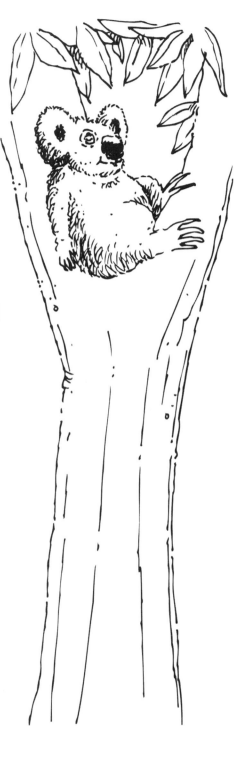

But the koala is a special kind of mammal. It is a marsupial. A female marsupial has a pouch on her underside. This is where she will carry her baby as it grows.

A newborn koala is tiny, blind, and hairless. It is only about the size of a lima bean, but it must crawl up into its mother's pouch. There it will eat, sleep, and grow for about six months. After that, the baby rides on its mother's back until it can take care of itself. But it will hop back into the pouch when it is sleepy or scared.

The koala feeds on the leaves of eucalyptus (gum) trees. It eats the tender shoots from the tips of the branches. Most of the water it needs also comes from these leaves. A koala has two sharp teeth in front for tearing the leaves or stripping bark. It has flat teeth in back for chewing the leaves.

The koala is a nocturnal animal. This means that it is active at night and sleeps most of the day. A koala doesn't have a home or a nest. It eats and sleeps in a tree, but it may go to the ground to move to a new tree. The koala just wedges its body into the fork of the tree. Then it wraps its arms or legs around a branch, closes its eyes, and goes to sleep.

Questions About *The Koala* ·

1. How is a koala the same as other mammals?

   _____

   _____

2. How is a koala different from other mammals?

   _____

3. Describe how a koala uses its teeth to eat.

   _____

   _____

4. How does a koala sleep if it doesn't have a nest or a burrow?

   _____

   _____

5. Why doesn't a male koala have a pouch?

   _____

Think About It ·

Read about the marsupials below. Then write a general statement about marsupials.

koala
- has two thumbs on each hand for climbing
- eats eucalyptus leaves
- is found in Australia

    _____

wombat
- has sharp claws for digging
- eats grass
- is found in Australia

    _____

kangaroo
- has large feet for hopping
- eats grass and low-growing plants
- is found in Australia

    _____

Skills: Recall information to answer questions; make inferences; make generalizations.

Read and Understand with Leveled Texts, Grade 3 • EMC 3443 • © Evan-Moor Corp.

What Does It Mean? ·

Use the correct word in each sentence.

| nocturnal | marsupials | mammal | eucalyptus |
| wedge | female | pouch | Australia |

1. A baby _____ drinks its mother's milk.

2. Only the _____ koala has babies.

3. At night, _____ animals become active.

4. A koala baby grows up in its mother's _____.

5. Koalas _____ themselves in the fork of a tree to sleep.

6. Animals that have pouches are _____.

7. The _____ is a kind of tree.

8. Most marsupials live in _____.

More Than One Meaning · · · · · · · · · · · · · · · · · ·

Fill in the circle next to the correct meaning.

1. In the story, **gum** means _____.

   Ⓐ a eucalyptus tree   Ⓑ something to chew

2. In the story, **fork** means _____.

   Ⓐ a tool to eat with   Ⓑ where two branches come together

3. In the story, **bark** means _____.

   Ⓐ the outside layer of a tree   Ⓑ the sound a dog makes

4. In the story, **shoots** means _____.

   Ⓐ fires a gun   Ⓑ tender new growth on a plant

Skills: Build vocabulary; practice words with multiple meanings.

Words into Syllables ●

A word that has two consonants in the middle is divided into syllables between the two consonants.

funnel = fun – nel   circus = cir – cus

Divide the words into syllables.

1. funny _____ – _____   5. only _____ – _____

2. tender _____ – _____   6. into _____ – _____

3. pencil _____ – _____   7. mammal _____ – _____

4. basket _____ – _____   8. active _____ – _____

Who Owns It? ●

mother's purse	only one owner – add **'s**
all birds' nests	more than one owner – add **s'**
children's lunches	irregular plural – add **'s**
its saddle	exception – add **s** only

Circle the missing word.

1. Put the letter on your _____ desk.   dad's   dads'

2. The kitten opened _____ eyes.   it's   its

3. All of the _____ bikes were blue.   boy's   boys'

4. Both _____ cars needed washing.   men's   mens'

Rewrite each phrase, using an apostrophe.

1. the pouch of a koala   _____

2. a letter to Mario   _____

3. cookies for the children   _____

4. a new leash for it   _____

5. the leader of a country   _____

6. toys belonging to the kittens   _____

Skills: Divide words into syllables; form singular and plural possessives.

Read and Understand with Leveled Texts, Grade 3 • EMC 3443 • © Evan-Moor Corp.

Compare the Mammals ·

Make check marks to show how a koala and a dog are alike and
how they are different.

	Koala	Dog	Both
1. The baby drinks its mother's milk.			
2. The baby grows inside its mother until birth.			
3. The mother protects the baby.			
4. The baby is born live.			
5. The baby is born before it is fully formed.			
6. The baby's body is covered with hair at birth.			
7. The newborn is the size of a lima bean at birth.			
8. The mother has many babies at one time.			

What Koalas Can Do ·

Circle the verbs in the list below. Then find them in the word search.

born   grow   carry

tear   tree   crawl

koala   eat   strip

feed   chew   wedge

slow   sleep   wrap

go   see   walk

pouch   climb   drink

```
c l i m b w r a p s w
r e s l e e p g d c a
a c a r r y x o r h l
w h s t r i p z i o k
l e s e e b i r n o w
q w e d g e f x k l y
t e a r g z f f e e d
```

Koala Crossword Puzzle

Use the words in the word box to complete the crossword puzzle.

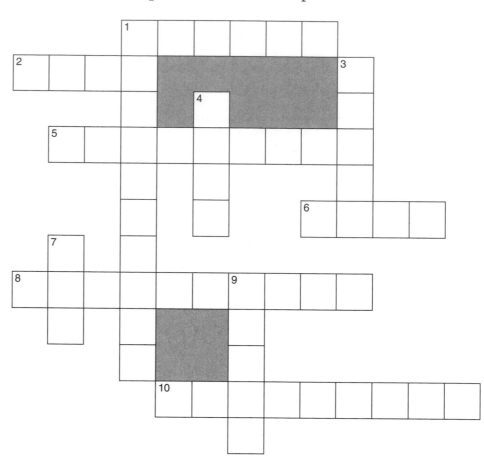

Word Box

Australia

bark

eucalyptus

gum

koala

lima

mammal

marsupials

nocturnal

pouch

tree

Across

1. an animal that feeds its own milk to its young
2. A newborn koala is the size of a ____ bean.
5. the country koalas come from
6. the outside covering of a tree
8. Koalas eat the leaves of this tree.
10. the name for animals that are active after dark

Down

1. mammals that have a pouch
3. a kind of marsupial
4. where a koala eats and sleeps
7. another name for the eucalyptus tree
9. where a female marsupial carries her baby

Skills: Use theme-related vocabulary to solve a crossword puzzle.

Read and Understand with Leveled Texts, Grade 3 • EMC 3443 • © Evan-Moor Corp.

Shannon Lucid – Astronaut

How would you feel if your mom went to outer space for six months? That's what happened to Shannon Lucid's children. Mrs. Lucid spent 188 days on the Russian space station Mir (meer). With two Russian cosmonauts, she made over 3,000 trips around Earth. She sent e-mail to her family every day. Her favorite snack, M&Ms, was sent up to her in space capsules.

Shannon Lucid was born in China, where her parents were American missionaries. After age six, she grew up in Oklahoma. Even as a child, she wanted to explore space. Later, she studied science in college. She also learned to fly a plane. These skills helped her become one of the first women astronauts.

Her project on Mir was to exercise. Being weightless for a long time can make bones and muscles weak. Some astronauts have to be carried off the shuttle after a long time in space. Doctors wanted to see if exercise would help keep their bodies strong.

Mrs. Lucid exercised for a couple of hours every day on Mir. When she came back to Earth, she was wobbly. But she was able to walk off the space shuttle. She had checkups over the next few years to keep looking for any changes in her bones and muscles.

What does Mrs. Lucid want to do next? She says she'd like to go to Mars!

Questions About *Shannon Lucid – Astronaut* · · · · · · · · · · ·

1. What is Mir? _____

2. Who was on board Mir with Shannon Lucid?

   _____

3. What does the story tell you about Shannon Lucid's childhood?

   _____

4. What skills helped her become an astronaut?

   _____

5. How did she keep in touch with her family while out in space?

   _____

6. What was her project on the space station?

   _____

7. Do you think Mrs. Lucid enjoyed her trip? Why or why not?

   _____

   _____

Think About It ·

What questions would you ask Shannon Lucid if you met her?

_____

_____

Would you like to be an astronaut someday?
Give at least two reasons for your answer.

_____

_____

Skills: Recall information to answer questions; make inferences; practice critical thinking.

Read and Understand with Leveled Texts, Grade 3 • EMC 3443 • © Evan-Moor Corp.

Name _____

What Does It Mean? ·

Write each word from the story next to its meaning.

astronaut   Mir   space station
cosmonaut   missionary   weightless
exercise   shuttle   wobbly

1. the Russian space station _____

2. an American space traveler _____

3. an aircraft made for travel into space _____

4. having no weight _____

5. a Russian space traveler _____

6. to use your body to get stronger _____

7. shaky or unsteady _____

8. a manned satellite orbiting Earth _____

9. a person who helps people in other
   lands and teaches them about religion _____

What Happened Next? ·

Complete the sentences to tell events in Shannon Lucid's life.

1. Shannon Lucid was born in _____.

2. She grew up in _____.

3. She studied _____.

4. She learned how to _____.

5. She was one of the first _____.

6. She spent 188 days _____.

7. Next, she would like to _____.

Skills: Build vocabulary; sequence story events.   **119**

Name _____

Beginning or Ending? •

Put a prefix at the beginning of a word to change its meaning.

pre = before   **un** = not

Put a suffix at the end of a word to change its meaning.

less = without   **ful** = filled with

Add a prefix or a suffix to make each word.

1. not able to _____able

5. not happy _____happy

2. filled with joy joy_____

6. see before _____view

3. without weight weight_____

7. very pretty beauti_____

4. before the game _____game

8. no money penni_____

Write a sentence for each of the new words you made.

1. _____

2. _____

3. _____

4. _____

5. _____

6. _____

7. _____

8. _____

Skill: Use prefixes (**pre** and **un**) and suffixes (**less** and **ful**).

Read and Understand with Leveled Texts, Grade 3 • EMC 3443 • © Evan-Moor Corp.

Space Adventure ·

Circle the verbs in the story below. Then write each verb in the correct box.

Alex climbed into the shuttle. He felt excited and worried
at the same time.

"What happens next?" he asked himself. He read the schedule
of procedures once more.

1. Put on spacesuit and pack equipment.

2. Examine shuttle and make sure everything works.

3. Fly to Zennox.

4. Collect rock samples.

5. Return to ship.

Alex smiled and started the engine. Then the shuttle blasted off.
Alex looked out the window and watched as Earth grew smaller and
smaller.

Travel to Zennox took three months. Alex exercised every day.
He wanted to be strong when he reached the distant planet. At last
he arrived!

Present Tense	**Past Tense**

Skills: Identify verbs; recognize and categorize verbs by tense.   121

Name _____

Dreams ···

Shannon Lucid dreamed of becoming a space explorer when she grew up. What do you dream of becoming? Tell why.

_____

_____

_____

_____

_____

Studying science and learning to fly a plane helped Shannon Lucid become an astronaut. What could you learn that will help you reach your dream?

_____

_____

_____

_____

_____

Read and Understand with Leveled Texts, Grade 3 • EMC 3443 • © Evan-Moor Corp.

Vampire Bats

Eli saw a scary movie on television last night. In the movie, a man turned into a vampire and attacked people to drink their blood. Eli woke up in the middle of the night screaming, "No! No! Don't suck my blood!" His father decided it was time to go to the library and find out the truth about vampires.

Eli learned that there are animals called vampire bats. These small bats drink blood, but they are not like the vampires in the movies. And they usually don't bite humans.

Vampire bats live in the warm, tropical parts of Central and South America. They sleep during the day. Then they come out at night to feed on the blood of other animals.

The hungry bat lands near a sleeping animal. It climbs onto its prey to feed. With its razor-sharp teeth, it makes a small incision on a bare part of the animal. It does not suck the blood up through fangs. It laps the blood up like a kitten laps up milk. The blood stays thin while the bat eats. A vampire bat has something in its saliva that keeps the blood from clotting.

There is one way vampire bats can be harmful. Many of them carry serious diseases, including rabies. As they eat, they can give these diseases to other animals.

So Eli learned two important things. First, people don't turn into bloodsucking vampires. And second, don't watch scary movies before going to bed. They can give you nightmares!

Questions About *Vampire Bats* ···

1. What caused Eli to have a nightmare?

   _____

2. What are five true things Eli learned about vampire bats? List them.

   a. _____

   b. _____

   c. _____

   d. _____

   e. _____

3. Why is it dangerous to handle wild animals, even small ones like vampire bats?

   _____

4. What do you think a person should do if bitten by a bat?

   _____

Think About It ···

Eli had a nightmare after watching a scary movie.
Write about a nightmare you have had and tell what you think caused it.

_____

_____

_____

_____

Skills: Recall information to answer questions; make inferences; practice critical thinking; write a personal narrative.

Read and Understand with Leveled Texts, Grade 3 • EMC 3443 • © Evan-Moor Corp.

Name _____

Vampire Bats

Long Vowel Sounds ·····················

Write the long vowel you hear in each word. Circle the letter or letter combination that makes the long vowel sound.

1. they _____   8. though _____

2. time _____   9. movie _____

3. scream _____   10. cute _____

4. night _____   11. cloak _____

5. go _____   12. fly _____

6. sleep _____   13. human _____

7. day _____   14. strain _____

List all the ways the long vowel sounds were spelled in the words above.

long a	long e	long i	long o	long u
_____	_____	_____	_____	_____
_____	_____	_____	_____	_____
_____	_____	_____	_____	_____

The Sound of *y* at the End ·····················

Say the words below. Write the letter that **y** sounds like in each word.

1. scary _____   4. happy _____

2. fly _____   5. my _____

3. carry _____   6. try _____

At the end of many one-syllable words, **y** says _____.

At the end of many two-syllable words, **y** says _____.

Read and Understand with Leveled Texts, Grade 3 • EMC 3443 • © Evan-Moor Corp.

Skills: Identify long vowel sounds; identify the sounds of **y** at the end of one- and two-syllable words.

Vampire Bats

What Does It Mean? •••••••••••••••••••••••••••••••••

Use the words in the word box to complete the crossword puzzle.

Word Box
bare
bat
blood
clot
decide
fang
incision
nightmare
rabies
saliva
serious
vampire

Down

1. a bat that drinks blood
2. a flying mammal
4. a disease of warmblooded animals
5. to make up your mind
7. a long, sharp tooth
8. a red fluid in the body

Across

3. a liquid in the mouth; spit
6. a frightening dream
8. not covered
9. a cut
10. important; needing thought
11. to become thick and stick together

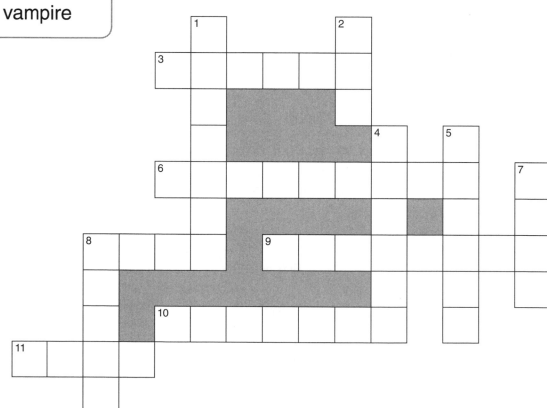

Skill: Use theme-related vocabulary to solve a crossword puzzle.

Read and Understand with Leveled Texts, Grade 3 • EMC 3443 • © Evan-Moor Corp.

Name _____

Fact or Fiction? ·

Write **true** or **false** after each statement.

1. Vampire bats drink blood.   _____

2. People can turn into vampires.   _____

3. You can learn about vampires at the library.   _____

4. Vampire bats suck blood up through their fangs.   _____

5. Vampire bats can carry diseases.   _____

6. Vampire bats have razor-sharp teeth.   _____

7. Vampire bats eat during the day and
   sleep when it is dark.   _____

8. A vampire bat's saliva makes blood stay
   thin so it is easier to drink.   _____

9. Vampire bats live all over the world.   _____

Draw a vampire bat.	Draw a vampire in a nightmare.

Skill: Distinguish between fact and fiction by identifying statements as true or false.   **127**

Alike and Different ••

Think of what you know about birds and about vampire bats.
How are they alike? How are they different? Write at least three facts
in each space on the diagram.

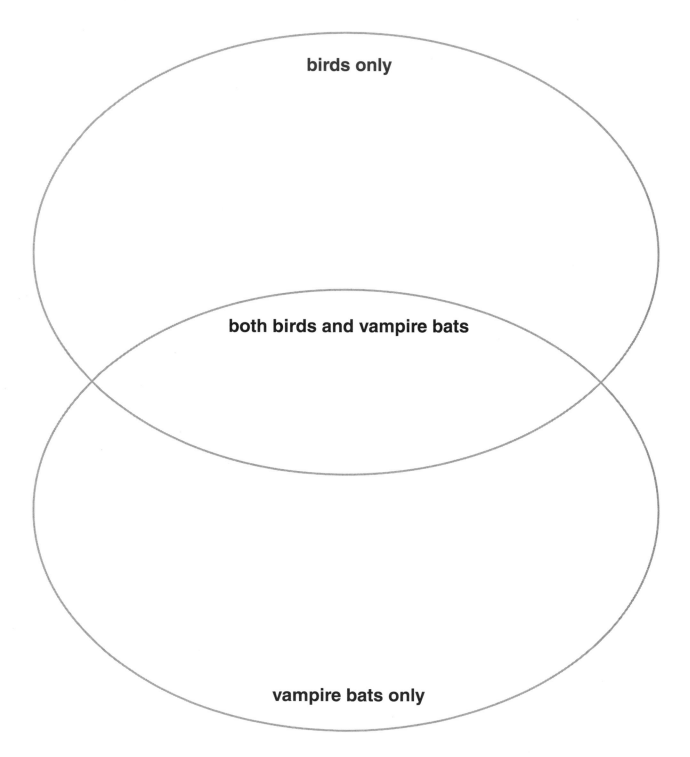

birds only

both birds and vampire bats

vampire bats only

Skill: Use prior knowledge to compare and contrast.

Read and Understand with Leveled Texts, Grade 3 • EMC 3443 • © Evan-Moor Corp.

George Washington Carver

What can you make out of peanuts? Most of us would think of peanut butter or peanut cookies. George Washington Carver didn't stop thinking until he had come up with more than one hundred things to make out of peanuts.

George was born in 1864. His mother was a slave. She was stolen when George was still a baby, so he was raised by her owners, Moses and Susan Carver.

All his life, George loved plants. At only seven years old, he already knew a lot about plants. He knew so much that people called him "the plant doctor."

George loved to learn, but there were no schools for black children where he lived. At age ten, he left home to find a town that let black children go to school. He went to schools in Missouri and Kansas until he finished high school. All that time, he had to earn a living. He worked as a cook, and he opened his own laundry.

When he went to college, Carver first studied art and music. But he still loved plants, so he began to study agriculture. After he graduated, the well-known inventor Thomas Edison asked him to work in his laboratory. But George had other plans. He became a teacher. In 1896, he was named head of the agriculture program at Tuskegee Institute in Alabama. It was a school that had been started for black students in 1881.

In those days, many farmers in the South grew cotton as their only crop. Always growing the same crop was hard on the soil. Soon, the cotton didn't grow well. Carver trained the farmers to grow other plants. Plants such as sweet potatoes and peanuts helped make the soil rich again. Before he died, in 1943, Carver invented hundreds of ways to use these two plants. He invented so many things that he was called "The Wizard of Tuskegee."

Questions About *George Washington Carver* · · · · · · · · · ·

1. Why was George raised by Moses and Susan Carver?

_____

2. What did George do at

seven years old? _____

ten years old? _____

3. After George finished college, who wanted him to work in his laboratory? Why did George say no?

_____

_____

4. How did George Washington Carver help southern farmers?

_____

_____

5. What did Carver do at Tuskegee Institute?

_____

6. How did Carver earn the nickname "The Wizard of Tuskegee"?

_____

Think About It ·

It was difficult for George Washington Carver to go to school when he was a boy. How would it be different for him if he were a boy today?

_____

_____

_____

Skills: Recall information to answer questions; make inferences; practice critical thinking.

Read and Understand with Leveled Texts, Grade 3 • EMC 3443 • © Evan-Moor Corp.

Name _____

What Does It Mean? ·

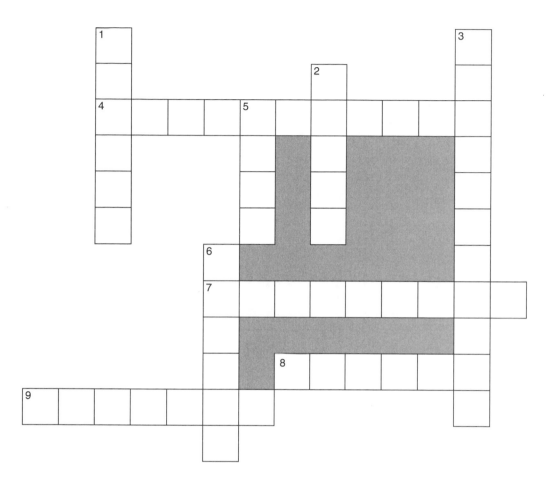

Word Box

agriculture

crop

institute

invent

laundry

peanut

slave

sweet potato

wizard

Down
1. the seed of one kind of plant
2. a person who is owned by someone
3. a type of vegetable
5. a type of plant that is grown on a farm
6. a very clever person

Across
4. farming
7. a place to study specialized subjects after high school
8. to create something new
9. a place where clothes are washed and ironed

Skills: Use theme-related vocabulary to solve a crossword puzzle.   **131**

The Sounds of *ow* ·

Say the words. Then write each word under the correct sound.

allow	crowd	own
below	flow	tow
brow	flower	town

ow　　　　　　　　　　　　　　　**ō**

_____　　_____

_____　　_____

_____　　_____

_____　　_____

_____　　_____

In the Past ·

Write the past tense for each verb.

run　_____　　grow　_____

keep　_____　　find　_____

begin　_____　　blow　_____

Use the words you made to fill in the blanks.

1. Many slaves _____ away from their owners.

2. Our neighbor _____ his car in our garage.

3. The flowers _____ to bloom in spring.

4. The farmers _____ peanuts and sweet potatoes.

5. The pirates _____ hidden treasure in a cave.

6. Toby _____ out the candles on his birthday cake.

Skills: Practice the sounds of **ow**; use irregular past tense verbs.

Read and Understand with Leveled Texts, Grade 3 • EMC 3443 • © Evan-Moor Corp.

Peanuts •

List all the ways that you have eaten peanuts or have seen peanuts used.

_____

_____

_____

_____

Made from Peanuts •

Find these products that George Washington Carver made from peanuts in the word search puzzle below. Then look at the word list again and draw a line under the products that you have used.

axle grease	shampoo	ice cream	plastic	soap
shoe polish	bleach	ink	rubber	milk
coffee	linoleum	salad oil	candy	dye

```
a c s h a m p o o b l
s h o e p o l i s h i
a o d f h c a n d y n
l r u b b e r k m l o
a m i p l a s t i c l
d y e p e o q s l n e
o u s o a p u w k v u
i a z i c e c r e a m
l e b d h c o f f e e
a x l e g r e a s e y
```

George Washington Carver ·

Write what you learned about the life of
George Washington Carver, in the order
it happened.

_____

_____

_____

_____

_____

_____

_____

_____

_____

How would you describe George Washington Carver?
Give reasons for your answer.

_____

_____

_____

_____

Read and Understand with Leveled Texts, Grade 3 • EMC 3443 • © Evan-Moor Corp.

Tornado!

Twister, cyclone, and tornado are all names for the same kind of storm. Whichever name you use, the storm is powerful and frightening. It can also cause a lot of damage.

Some of the clouds in the storm grow very large. Then they form a funnel shape. The funnel is thick and dark. It forms when cold air rushes up under warm air. The warm air is lighter, so it rises quickly and spins around. As the tornado twists, storm winds push it across land. At times, the small end of the funnel touches the ground. Usually, the storm also brings lightning, thunder, and heavy rain.

The center of the tornado causes the most damage. The air pressure inside the funnel is much lower than the outside pressure. The difference in pressure makes the tornado act like a giant vacuum cleaner. It can pull up trees by their roots and toss cars into the air. It can rip the roofs off buildings. A building caught by the center of the funnel can explode.

People who live where tornadoes happen need a safe place to go during the storm. Many homes have underground storm cellars. The family can stay there until the tornado passes.

Almost all tornadoes happen in the United States. They happen most often during spring and early summer. Storm watchers warn people when weather conditions could cause a tornado. But no one can tell ahead of time exactly where it will touch down.

Read and Understand with Leveled Texts, Grade 3 • EMC 3443 • © Evan-Moor Corp.

Questions About *Tornado!* ·

1. What is a tornado?

_____

2. Describe a tornado's shape.

_____

3. What are two other names for a tornado?

_____

4. How is a tornado like a giant vacuum cleaner?

_____

5. What kinds of damage does a tornado cause when it touches the ground?

_____

6. Fill in the circles next to the ways to be safe during a tornado.

   ○ Run around and scream.   ○ Go to a storm cellar.
   ○ Stay away from windows.   ○ Listen to a battery radio.
   ○ Stand under a big tree.   ○ Get in a car and drive away.

Think About It ·

What do people do to help each other after a tornado has done its damage? Include at least three things.

_____

_____

_____

Skills: Recall information to answer questions; draw conclusions; practice critical thinking.

Read and Understand with Leveled Texts, Grade 3 • EMC 3443 • © Evan-Moor Corp.

What Does It Mean? ·

Match each word with its meaning.

pressure •   • harm

explode •   • the force of air on a surface

lightning •   • a loud sound caused by lightning

damage •   • an underground room

clouds •   • to blow up

thunder •   • a place

cellar •   • electric flashes in the sky

location •   • a large group of water drops in the air

Riddles ·

Write and draw the answer to each riddle.

I am a machine used to clean carpets. What am I?

_____

I flash across the sky during a bad storm. What am I?

_____

Skill: Build vocabulary.   **137**

Letters That Say *aw* ·

aw	**ough**	**ol**	**al**
raw	bought	follow	fall

Fill in the missing letters.

1. I want to c_____ my grandfather on his birthday.

2. The wild dogs f_____ over the bones.

3. There is a squirrel's nest in that h_____ tree.

4. Dad used a s_____ to cut the log.

5. Tony bounced his b_____ against a brick w_____.

6. We heard the crows c_____ outside our window.

Base Words ·

Write the base word on the line.

1. tornadoes   _____

2. lighter   _____

3. touches   _____

4. dried   _____

5. passes   _____

6. scary   _____

7. flies   _____

8. exploding   _____

9. hurried   _____

10. rises   _____

Skills: Practice letter combinations that make the /aw/ sound; identify base words.

Read and Understand with Leveled Texts, Grade 3 • EMC 3443 • © Evan-Moor Corp.

Natural Disasters ···

A natural disaster is an event that causes a lot of damage. A tornado is one kind of natural disaster. The list of words below names other natural disasters. Find each word in the puzzle and circle it. Make a check mark next to the word when you find it.

_____ blizzard

_____ drought

_____ earthquake

_____ fire

_____ flood

_____ hailstorm

_____ heat wave

_____ hurricane

_____ landslide

_____ volcano

```
h  u  r  r  i  c  a  n  e  f  l
e  a  r  t  h  q  u  a  k  e  a
a  r  i  b  a  u  s  w  n  r  n
t  c  b  l  i  z  z  a  r  d  d
w  t  o  u  s  a  l  z  k  r  s
a  f  i  r  e  t  w  v  f  o  l
v  o  l  c  a  n  o  d  q  u  i
e  a  r  o  g  h  t  r  o  g  d
u  m  t  l  o  v  i  q  m  h  e
m  y  h  w  b  d  r  u  j  t  v
```

Stormy Weather ···

What kinds of storms or other natural disasters happen where you live? Describe the damage they cause.

_____

_____

_____

_____

_____

Skills: Use visual discrimination to find theme-related vocabulary in a word search puzzle; write a descriptive personal narrative.

Tornado in a Jar ·····················

Read the directions. Then answer the questions.

Materials:
a jar with a lid
water
liquid detergent
small objects (pebble, game piece, button)

Steps to Follow:
1. Fill the jar almost to the top with water.
2. Add 1/4 cup of liquid detergent and the small objects.
3. Put the lid on the jar securely.
4. Hold the jar with both hands and shake it in a circular motion.
5. Watch the tornado appear.

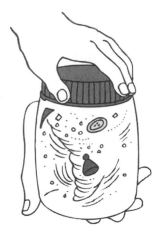

1. How many materials do you need?

   _____

2. What do you do after you put water into the jar?

   _____

3. What happens when you shake the jar in a circular motion?

   _____

4. Why do you put small objects into the jar?

   _____

Now collect your materials and make your own "tornado in a jar."

Skills: Read and follow directions; make inferences.

Read and Understand with Leveled Texts, Grade 3 • EMC 3443 • © Evan-Moor Corp.

Comparing Texts

Along with building background and activating prior knowledge or experience, comparing texts is an important reading strategy that aids and improves reading comprehension. The focus of this reading strategy is making connections. In comparing texts, students make text-to-text connections based on what they read.

Comparing texts is a heavily tested reading objective that promotes both literary analysis and critical-thinking skills. By making text-to-text connections, students

- learn how to compare and contrast literary elements such as characters, plot, theme, and setting;
- better understand individual texts by seeing them juxtaposed with one another; and
- practice higher order critical and creative thinking.

The activities on the following pages ask students to think about two stories and then answer questions that compare the texts. The activities are suitable for both group instruction and independent practice (see page 4). Before comparing the texts, students must have read both of the stories and should have completed some or all of their related skill pages.

The Wise Old Woman and *The Tortoise and the Hare*

1. A fable is a story that has a moral, or lesson.
   Write what you think the moral is of each story.

   The Wise Old Woman: _____

   _____

   The Tortoise and the Hare: _____

   _____

2. Name the character or characters in each story who learned
   the lesson. Explain how the character learned the lesson.

   The Wise Old Woman: _____

   _____

   The Tortoise and the Hare: _____

   _____

3. Name the character in each story who taught the lesson. Tell how.

   The Wise Old Woman: _____

   _____

   The Tortoise and the Hare: _____

   _____

4. Which story did you like better? Tell why.

   _____

   _____

Read and Understand with Leveled Texts, Grade 3 • EMC 3443 • © Evan-Moor Corp.

The Messiest Room in Town and *The Dog Ate My Homework*

1. What was the lesson that both stories were trying to teach?

   _____

2. At the end of each story, which character or characters learned the lesson? How do you know?

   _____

   _____

3. Which story could <u>not</u> happen in real life? Tell why.

   _____

   _____

4. Compare the story endings. Was each ending happy or not happy? Circle the answer and explain why you think that.

   The Messiest Room in Town   happy   not happy

   _____

   The Dog Ate My Homework   happy   not happy

   _____

5. Which story did you like better? Tell why.

   _____

   _____

A Grasshopper's Life Cycle and The Koala

1. How are these two stories alike? Name two ways.

   _____

   _____

2. Read the facts below about each animal's young.
   Then write the facts where they belong in the diagram.

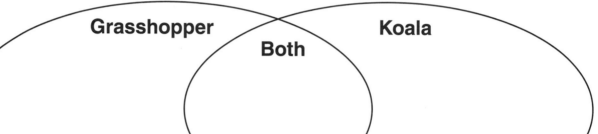

   molts   needs food   does not look like an adult

   born live   tiny as a lima bean hatches from an egg

   Grasshopper   **Koala**
                  Both

3. Which story tells about something that
   this diagram would help you show?

   ○ *A Grasshopper's Life Cycle*
   ○ *The Koala*

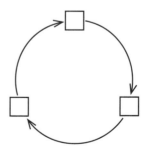

4. Which story did you like better? Tell why.

   _____

   _____

Read and Understand with Leveled Texts, Grade 3 • EMC 3443 • © Evan-Moor Corp.

The Fisherman and His Wife and *Daedalus and Icarus*

1. Who wanted too much in each story? Write the character's name.
   Then tell what the character wanted to do that was too much.

   The Fisherman and His Wife: _____

   _____

   Daedalus and Icarus: _____

   _____

2. How was the sea important in each story?

   _____

   _____

3. Write the names of the characters under the correct headings.

   Icarus   fisherman   Daedalus   fisherman's wife   fish

gives instructions	always follows instructions	does <u>not</u> always follow instructions
_____	_____	_____
_____	_____	_____
_____	_____	_____

4. Which story did you like better? Tell why.

   _____

   _____

When Granny Met Johnny Appleseed and George Washington Carver

1. Which story does each clue tell about?
   Write the correct title on the line.

   This story is about a person's life.

   _____

   This story is about one day in a person's life.

   _____

   This story is told by someone who is in the story.

   _____

   This story is told by someone who is <u>not</u> in the story.

   _____

2. Read each story detail and make an **X** in the correct box.

	Appleseed	Carver	Both
worked in the South			
traveled west			
helped people grow plants for food			
was called "the plant doctor"			
loved to grow things			

3. Which story could you use for information if you were writing a report about a famous person? Why?

   _____

   _____

Read and Understand with Leveled Texts, Grade 3 • EMC 3443 • © Evan-Moor Corp.

Answer Key

Page 7
1. squeaky, shiny, creaky
2. leaky, brown
3. The old shoes leaked. **or**
   The old shoes were worn out.
4. Answers will vary but might include:
   They were more comfortable.
   He liked the way they looked.
   They were his favorite shoes.
5. creaky, leaky

Page 8

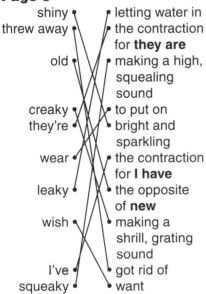

Answers will vary but might include:

boots	sneakers
slippers	sandals
skates	socks

Page 9

threw	three	thrush
throat	thread	threat
through	thrill	throb

1. throat
2. threw
3. thread
4. through
5. three
6. thrush

1. peak
2. sneak
3. beak
4. weak
5. squeak
6. leak
7. speak
8. creak

Page 10
1. bear
2. scent
3. flee
4. through
5. bury
6. rain
7. byte
8. dough
9. maize

1. rain
2. bear / berries
3. knew
4. sow
5. dough
6. board
7. heel
8. sent

Page 11
Drawings and answers will vary.

Page 14
1. She lived at the edge of the woods.
2. She walked down the path and across the woods.
3. She met a wolf, a snake, and a bear.
   They wanted to eat her.
4. She ate and took a nap.
5. She wanted the pumpkin to hide in.
6. Answers will vary but should include some of the following points:
   She tricked the animals into letting her go to her son's house.
   She hid in the pumpkin so the animals couldn't see her.
   She got the animals to fight with each other so she could run away.
   Answers will vary but should include:
   Animals can't talk to people.

Page 15

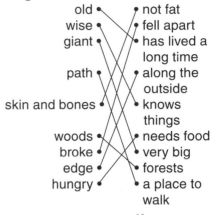

woman	**wolf**
old	bushy-tailed
skin and bones	hungry
wise	gray

snake	**bear**
hungry	big
green	black
long	hungry

Page 16
1. g
2. j
3. g
4. g
5. j
6. g
7. j
8. g

gum	jam jar	giant
jacks	gorilla	jeep

1. son**'s**
2. woman**'s**
3. wolf**'s**
4. pumpkin**'s**
5. tree**'s**
6. bear**'s**

Page 17
1. The old woman filled a basket with cookies.
2. "When I come back from my son's house, I will be fatter," she said.
3. The old woman ate and took a nap at her son's house.
4. The old woman got into the pumpkin and rolled into the woods.
5. The pumpkin rolled past the bear, the snake, and the wolf.
6. The giant pumpkin hit a big tree and broke open.
7. While the animals were fighting, the old woman ran home.

Page 18
1. B   2. C   3. A

Drawings look like the animals.

Page 21
1. Answers will vary but should include some of the following: It was littered with toys and clothes.

   There was stuff under the bed. Rotten, moldy food and pet hair were all over the floor.
2. Dirty clothes, rotten apple cores, and moldy pizza made it smell bad.
3. The dust monster wanted Herbert to clean his room.
4. It didn't want to smell the dirty clothes and rotten food.
5. Answers will vary.
6. Answers will vary but should include the idea that Herbert threw things around and never put anything away.

Answers will vary.

Page 22

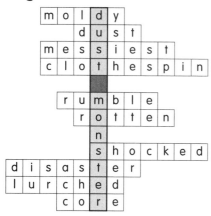

A **dust monster** is hiding under the bed!

Page 23

a	**e**	**i**	**o**	**u**
can	get	ring	dollar	pup
that	bed	still	pocket	hush
glass	tell	sing	rock	tug
rattle	rest	in	bottle	of

1. smaller   smallest
2. messier   messiest
3. funnier   funniest
4. sillier   silliest
5. faster   fastest
6. tinier   tiniest

Page 24
1–4

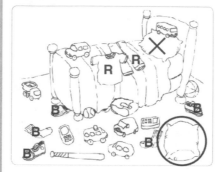

5. Apple core and half-eaten pizza are drawn somewhere on the floor.
6. **11** toys
7. Answers will vary.

Page 25
Drawings will vary but must include the items mentioned in each sentence.

Page 27
1. Female grasshoppers lay their eggs in a hole in the ground in fall.
2. They are called nymphs.
3. A grasshopper **molts** when it grows too big for its skin.
4. nymph   adult   egg
5. It is a cycle because it happens over and over again. **or**
   It is a cycle because the eggs are laid, the nymphs hatch, they grow up, more eggs are laid, and then it all starts again.

Answers will vary but should include the following stages:
   baby
   child
   adult

Page 28
   2 1 4 3
1. An egg is laid.
2. A nymph with no wings hatches from the egg.
3. The nymph gets bigger and grows wings.
4. The grasshopper is fully grown.

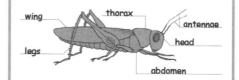

Page 29

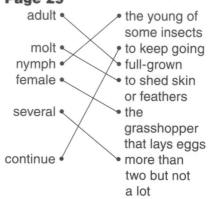

1. B   2. C   3. A

Page 30
finger   cal**f**   tele**ph**one
nym**ph**   coffee   al**ph**abet

laid   came
ate   made
hatched   molted
grew   began
sent   slept

1. sent
2. laid
3. molted / grew
4. ate / came
5. slept / made

Page 31
1. fact
2. opinion
3. fact
4. fact
5. opinion
6. opinion
7. fact

cowgirl   peanut
sunflowers   applesauce
bunkhouse   Grasshopper
breakfast   rainbow
pancakes   sunshine

Page 33
1. Corn, Bean, Squash
2. She is tall, golden, graceful, and strong.
3. She twines around Corn.
4. Squash protects Corn and Bean.
5. The sisters change into young girls, and they dance and sing.
6. Answers will vary but should include one or more of the following:
   Corn, beans, and squash can be planted together in a garden.
   Vegetable plants can grow.
   Bean plants can twine around a cornstalk.
   Corn can be tall and strong.
   Squash grows close to the ground.
7. Answers will vary but should include one or more of the following:
   Beans, corn, and squash are not really sisters.
   Plants can't turn into girls.
   Plants can't dance.

Answers will vary but should contain information similar to the following:
   Some plants grow well together. **or**
   Some plants can help each other grow.

Page 34
1. Native Americans
2. sisters
3. graceful
4. twine
5. protect
6. praise
7. mound
8. moonlit

Corn, Bean, Squash

Page 35

see	bean	weak
fleas	clean	three
seed	feet	please

1. see / three
2. clean
3. fleas
4. bean / seeds

wanted   planted   loved   stayed

Sentences will vary.

Page 36

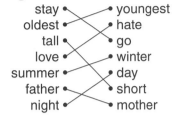

stay — youngest
oldest — hate
tall — go
love — winter
summer — day
father — short
night — mother

circled	X
small – little	come – go
below – under	fat – thin
happy – jolly	awake – asleep
sad – unhappy	late – early
scared – afraid	work – play
	dirty – clean
	wet – dry

Page 37
1. You can plant them close together.
2. Answers will vary.
3. Drawings will vary.

Page 39
1. Kim had not done her homework all week.
2. She could be at the park playing ball and then going to Jiffy Burger for lunch.
3. Her brother could have ripped up her homework.
   She could have been sick.
4. Answers will vary.
5. Answers will vary.

Cause: Kim had not done her homework all week.
Effect: Kim's mother put her on restriction.

Page 40
1. restriction
2. drain
3. explain
4. homework
5. trouble
6. groan

1. I'll
2. didn't
3. won't
4. that's
5. couldn't
6. where's

1. They're / their
2. You're / your
3. it's / its

Page 41

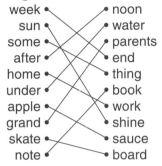

week — noon
sun — water
some — parents
after — end
home — thing
under — book
apple — work
grand — shine
skate — sauce
note — board

Drawings look like the words.

Page 42
1. harmless
2. teacher
3. joyful
4. sadly
5. homeless
6. careful
7. singer
8. quickly

1. rest   less
2. slow   ly
3. play   er
4. nice   ly
5. wonder   ful
6. care   less
7. dream   er

Page 43
Answers will vary but must retell the story in sequence.

Page 46

1. Papa was going to California to find work.
2. They packed pots, pans, clothes, and tools in the trunk.
3. She didn't want to go without her kitten, Skeeter.
4. She understood that Laura was unhappy about leaving her home and her pet.
5. Answers will vary but should include some of the following points:

   Mama explained why they had to go.

   She said that they would make a new home in California.

   Aunt Lizzie would take good care of Skeeter.

   They would come back for a visit someday.
6. They needed money for the trip.

Reasons will vary.

Page 47

1. mutter
2. huddle
3. cling
4. porch
5. choice
6. determined

1. A   2. B   3. C

Page 48

ways of speaking
explained
cried
muttered
whispered

proper names
Lizzie
Laura
Skeeter

parts of a car
back seat
roof
trunk

family members
aunt
brother
parents
sister

Page 49

circled

open	know	whole
hello	foam	load
stone	joke	piano
throat	mower	owner

o-e	open syllable	oa	ow
stone	open	throat	know
joke	hello	foam	mower
whole	piano	load	owner

ed	d	t
headed	begged	washed
wanted	planned	cooked
hunted	traveled	baked
planted	played	picked

Page 50

Problem:
They had a flat tire and didn't have a spare.
Solution:
Papa took the tire to a garage to be fixed.

Problem:
They needed money for gas and food.
Solution:
A farmer paid them to pick corn.

Problem:
Dog ran away.
Solution:
A man found him and brought him back.

Page 52

1. His leg and arm muscles are weak, and he's in a wheelchair.
2. Answers will vary but could include:

   He picked up things.

   He pulled the wheelchair.

   He opened doors.

   He pushed elevator buttons.

   He turned lights on and off.

   He carried things in a backpack.
3. Pete went to school for two years.
4. Harry had to learn how to give Pete commands and how to take care of him.
5. Pete has to be able to listen to Harry and to do what Harry needs.
6. seeing service dogs: blind people

   hearing service dogs: deaf people

Characters: Harry, Pete
Problem: Harry is in a wheelchair and can't do many things for himself.
Solution: Harry gets help from Pete, a service dog.

Page 53

taught
trained
tasks
service dogs
wheelchairs
problems

1. animal
2. see
3. day
4. swim
5. drink
6. small
7. out
8. lie on

Page 54

stays	knows	drops
pushes	opens	takes
picks	uses	washes

1. stays
2. takes
3. opens
4. knows
5. pushes
6. uses
7. washes
8. picks / drops

1. carries
2. flies
3. hurries
4. cries
5. worries
6. studies
7. tries
8. buries

Page 55

book		school	
look	brook	smooth	balloon
good	hook	loose	goose
cookie	stood	shampoo	soon

1. closed   opened
2. work   play
3. easy   difficult
4. answer   question
5. pulled   pushed
6. learn   teach
7. under   over
8. laughing   crying

Page 56

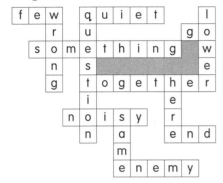

Page 58

1. Papa
2. Answers will vary but could include:
   To help the baby go to sleep.
   To make the baby stop crying.
   To make the baby happy.
3. mockingbird
   diamond ring
   looking glass
   billy goat
   cart and bull
   dog named Rover
   horse and cart
4. A diamond ring might turn brass.
   A looking glass might break.
   A cart and bull might turn over.
   Rover the dog might not bark.
5. sweetest, little

Answers will vary.

Page 59

1. mockingbird
2. brass
3. ring
4. town
5. bull

Answers in second column will vary.

rhyme	do not rhyme
(circled)	(X)
brass–glass	over–cover
you–shoe	bark–cart
fell–bell	come–home
buy–fly	broke–goat
	papa–saw

do n**o**t
you will
will n**o**t
Papa is
cannot
is n**o**t
they a**r**e

The snack is **popcorn**.

Page 60

kite	tie	cry
dime	pie	fry

1. small**est**
   small**er**
2. fast**er**
   fast**est**
3. tall**er**
   tall**est**

Page 61

1. diamond ring   4. buy
2. mockingbird   5. cart
3. billy goat   6. looking glass

top row: mockingbird, horse and cart, baby

bottom row: diamond ring, looking glass, billy goat

Page 62

Answers will vary.

Lists will vary.

Page 65

1. He went to the sea to fish.
2. The fish was magic (*or* an enchanted prince). **or** The fish could talk.
3. She kept wanting more things.
4. The fisherman had saved his life. **or** The fisherman had put him back into the water.
5. The fish was angry because the fisherman's wife wanted too much (*or* was greedy). The fish took back everything he had given to the fisherman and his wife.
6. greedy
7. Don't be greedy.

Answers will vary.

Page 66

1. Once upon a time, there lived a poor fisherman and his wife.
2. The fisherman caught an enchanted fish.
3. His wife sent him to ask for a cottage.
4. His wife sent him to ask for a castle.
5. His wife wanted to rule the world.
6. His wife wanted to control day and night.
7. The angry fish shouted, "You ask for too much!"
8. The couple were back in their old hut.

Page 67

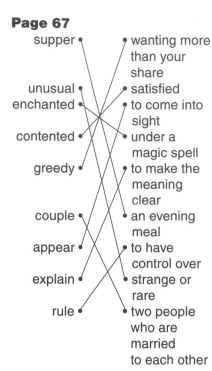

supper • • wanting more than your share

unusual • • satisfied

enchanted • • to come into sight

contented • • under a magic spell

greedy • • to make the meaning clear

couple • • an evening meal

appear • • to have control over

explain • • strange or rare

rule • • two people who are married to each other

Drawings look like the words.

Page 68
s   k
s   k
s   s
k   k
s   k
k   s

unusual   **un**comfortable
unhappy

Sentences will vary.

Page 69
Two-syllable words:
Answers will vary.

Three-syllable words (any five of the following): fisherman, enchanted, kindhearted, excited, demanded, unhappy, contented

Four-syllable words: vegetables, unusual

could really happen (any three)
The man could go fishing.
The woman could grow vegetables.
The couple could live by the sea.
The wife could be greedy.

make-believe (any three)
The fish was magic.
The fish could talk.
The fish could grant wishes.
The wife could rule the world.

Page 72
1. He was complaining that being the middle child wasn't fair. **or**
He was complaining that his big sister and little brother got to do things that he didn't get to do. **or**
He didn't like being the middle child.
2. Answers will vary (any three from the story list).
3. Answers will vary (any three from the story list).

Answers will vary, but sister's age should be 12 to early teens, and little brother's age should be in the baby to toddler range.

Page 73
1. B
2. A and C
3. C
4. B
5. B
6. A, B, and C

Sentences will vary.

Page 74
listen   **write**   **k**nit
talk   clim**b**   si**g**n

1. wrote / signed
2. climbed
3. knitted
4. listened / talked

ight   **old**
fight   bold
light   cold
night   fold
sight   told
tight   mold

Page 75
I can do it.
fly a kite
stay overnight with a friend
play soccer
fix my own breakfast
use in-line skates

I am too young.
drive a car
stay out until midnight
work in an office
go to R-rated movies
rent an apartment

Page 76
Answers will vary.

Page 79
1. Owl started the race.
2. He stopped to take a nap.
3. **circled:** steady, poky, slow-moving, well-liked
X: quick, foolish, embarrassed, unkind, showoff
4. Keep trying and you will succeed.

Answers will vary.

Page 80
1. tortoise
2. congratulated
3. embarrassed
4. crept
5. hare
6. steadily
7. boasted

1. winter
2. quickly
3. cried
4. finish
5. behind
6. sunny
7. loudly
8. lost

Page 81
bow   goat   bone
sew   hoe   globe
zero   toast   arrow

f   silent
f   silent
silent   silent
f   f

Page 82
1. slowly
2. steadily
3. happily
4. angrily

1. sleepily   4. handily
2. suddenly   5. quickly
3. loudly   6. prettily

Sentences will vary.

Page 83

Answers will vary.
Examples:

Hare: I want to show everyone that I am the fastest animal in the world.

Hare: Tortoise doesn't have a chance. He's the slowest animal there is.

Tortoise: Hare boasts about how fast he is, but I will outsmart him.

Tortoise: I plan to move steadily, without stopping, the whole race.

Tortoise: I knew I had won when I saw Hare taking a nap.

Page 85

1. Aunt Gertie likes to try new things. **or**
   Aunt Gertie likes adventures.
2. Answers may vary.
   Example:
   You might see fish and underwater plants.
3. snorkel: goes in your mouth and lets in air so you can breathe underwater

   face mask: keeps water out of your nose and eyes

   fins: adds power when kicking your feet as you swim
4. so you will know how to do it safely

Answers and reasons will vary.

Page 86

places: airport, hotel, Hawaiian Islands, sports center

what you wear when you're snorkeling: face mask, fins, snorkel, swimsuit

actions: breathe, dive, snorkel, kick, swim

mask   snorkel   fins

Page 87

dive
climb
dry
buy
high
fly
Islands

1. fins
2. classes
3. berries
4. men
5. books
6. dishes
7. babies
8. Islands
9. beaches
10. women
11. bunnies
12. jets
13. children
14. houses
15. geese
16. stories

Page 88

1. Aunt Gertie said, "Let's have an adventure."
2. We took classes to learn how to use the equipment.
3. We bought snorkels, face masks, and fins.
4. Aunt Gertie and I flew to the Hawaiian Islands.
5. We changed into our swimsuits and headed for the beach.
6. Aunt Gertie is grinning again. What will her next adventure be?

Page 89

1. (red circle) 6 lessons: $50
2. (blue box) Markham Sports Center
3. (green line) under "Saturday" (two green lines) under "8:00–10:00 a.m."
4. Answers will vary.

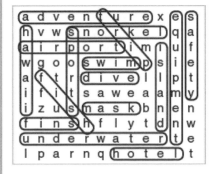

Page 92

1. A reptile has dry, scaly skin; lays eggs; and is coldblooded.
2. Reptiles can't make heat to keep their bodies warm on cold days. They have to live in a place that is warm to stay warm.
3. Answers will vary (any three of the following):
   Their eyes and nostrils are on the tops of their heads.

   They can close their nostrils to keep out water.

   They have a transparent flap covering each eye, so they can see underwater.

   Their bodies look like logs when they lie still in the water, making it easy for them to hide.
4. When their teeth fall out, they grow new ones right away. **or**
   They can grow fifty or more sets of teeth in a lifetime.
5. The mother can hear the babies making noises inside their shells.

Answers will vary.

Page 93

1. B
2. A
3. B
4. A, B, and C
5. C

coldblooded: not able to make body heat

hatchling: a baby animal that has hatched from an egg

transparent: clear (You can see through it.)

Page 94

wat**er** b**ir**d t**ur**n w**or**d **ear**n

My mot**her** is a n**ur**se. H**er** w**or**k is very important. Last Friday aft**er**noon, she left w**or**k **ear**ly so we could go to the movies togeth**er**. But f**ir**st, we ate at the pizza parl**or** next to the movie theat**er**.

The movie was about a gigantic monst**er** that was cov**er**ed with f**ur**. The monst**er** went around frightening everyone on **ear**th.

an	a	an
a	an	a
an	a	an
a	an	a

Page 95

1. hard
2. happy
3. small
4. slow
5. night
6. safe
7. warm
8. full
9. light
10. asleep
11. cooked
12. clean

crossed out:

toes	bird	pond
release	ribbon	table

Page 96

	Alligator	Crocodile
how it moves on land	moves along on its stomach with legs spread out at its sides	moves quickly with front and back legs working together
shape of snout	round and wide	narrow
position of teeth	two lower teeth don't show	two lower teeth show when mouth is closed
nest material and location	piles up a mound of plant material and mud for a nest	digs a nest in the sand

Page 99

1. King Minos controlled the land and the sea.
2. The wings were made of wax and feathers tied onto a wooden frame.
3. He needed to see how they moved their wings and how they hovered on air currents.
4. He flew too near the sun, and the sun's heat melted the wax and made the feathers fall off his wings.
5. Icarus wouldn't have fallen from the sky if he had followed his father's instructions.
6. Crete and Sicily

Answers will vary.

Page 100

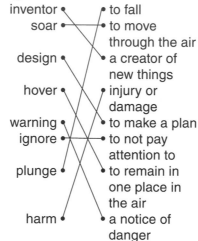

inventor — a creator of new things
soar — to move through the air
design — to make a plan
hover — to remain in one place in the air
warning — a notice of danger
ignore — to not pay attention to
plunge — to fall
harm — injury or damage

1. to
2. two
3. too

Sentences will vary.

Page 101

1. o͝o
2. ō
3. ow
4. ŭ
5. o͞o
6. aw
7. ow
8. ō
9. ow
10. ŭ
11. ow
12. aw
13. o͝o
14. ō
15. o͞o
16. ŭ

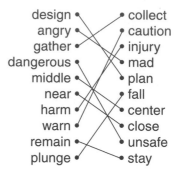

design — injury
angry — mad
gather — collect
dangerous — caution
middle — center
near — fall
harm — plan
warn — unsafe
remain — stay
plunge — close

Page 102

1. moving, moved
   hoping, hoped
   smiling, smiled
   moves
   hopes
   smiles

2. hopped, hopping
   controlled, controlling
   planned, planning
   hops
   controls
   plans

3. hurries, hurried
   studies, studied
   buries, buried
   hurrying
   studying
   burying

Page 103

Daedalus had to find a way to leave the island.

Daedalus designed wings to fly off the island.

The wax melted, and he fell into the sea and drowned.

Drawings show what the sentences describe.

Page 106
1. The children had been good all day.
2. They were headed west.
3. She followed a rabbit into the woods.
4. He was strange-looking (*or* funny-looking). **or** He was dressed in old, worn-out clothes, his feet were bare, and he had on a funny hat.
5. She wasn't afraid, because he had a kind smile and a twinkle in his eyes.
6. People started calling him Johnny Appleseed because, everywhere he went, he gave people apple seeds to plant.
7. Granny planted them with the seeds Johnny Appleseed gave her.
8. Answers will vary.

Answers will vary.

Page 107
1. traveling
2. staying
3. following
4. raising
5. wishing
6. going

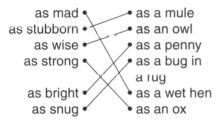

as mad • • as a mule
as stubborn • • as an owl
as wise • • as a penny
as strong • • as a bug in a rug
as bright • • as a wet hen
as snug • • as an ox

Similes will vary.
  Examples:
    as big as a house
    as cold as ice
    as fast as a jack rabbit
    as old as the hills

Page 108
1. A
2. C
3. B
4. B
5. A
6. C
7. C

Page 109
1. raise
2. table
3. player
4. plane

5. afraid
6. space
7. crayon
8. mayor

1. She
2. him
3. it
4. They

5. them
6. He
7. us
8. We

Page 110
Sources, answers, and drawings will vary.

Page 112
1. It has fur. Its babies are born live and drink milk from the mother.
2. A female koala has a pouch where she raises her baby.
3. A koala uses its sharp front teeth to tear off leaves or strip bark. It uses its flat back teeth to chew its food.
4. The koala wedges itself into the fork of a tree and wraps its arms or legs around a branch.
5. Male koalas don't need pouches because they don't have babies.

Several kinds of marsupials live in Australia. **or** Marsupials eat plants

Page 113
1. mammal
2. female
3. nocturnal
4. pouch
5. wedge
6. marsupials
7. eucalyptus
8. Australia

1. A
2. B
3. A
4. B

Page 114
1. fun-ny
2. ten-der
3. pen-cil
4. bas-ket

5. on-ly
6. in-to
7. mam-mal
8. ac-tive

1. dad's
2. its
3. boys'
4. men's

1. koala's pouch
2. Mario's letter
3. children's cookies
4. its new leash
5. country's leader
6. kittens' toys

Page 115
1. both
2. both
3. both
4. both

5. koala
6. dog
7. koala
8. dog

The only words **not** circled are: born, koala, slow, pouch, tree

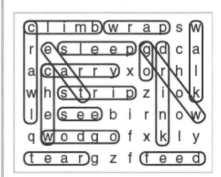

Page 116

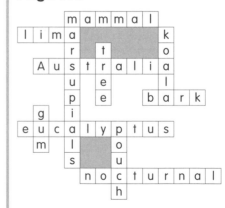

Page 118

1. a Russian space station
2. two Russian cosmonauts
3. Answers will vary but could include:
   She was born in China.
   Her parents were missionaries.
   She grew up in Oklahoma.
   She wanted to be a space explorer.
4. She studied science in college, and she learned to fly a plane.
5. She sent them e-mail messages every day.
6. She exercised every day to see if it would keep her bones and muscles strong.
7. Yes. She wants to go to Mars.

Questions will vary.

Answers will vary.

Page 119

1. Mir
2. astronaut
3. shuttle
4. weightless
5. cosmonaut
6. exercise
7. wobbly
8. space station
9. missionary

1. China
2. Oklahoma
3. science in college
4. fly a plane
5. women astronauts
6. on the Mir space station
7. go to Mars

Page 120

1. **u**nable
2. joy**ful**
3. weight**less**
4. **pre**game
5. **un**happy
6. **pre**view
7. beauti**ful**
8. penni**less**

Sentences will vary.

Page 121

Alex climbed into the shuttle. He felt excited and worried at the same time.

"What happens next?" he asked himself. He read the schedule of procedures once more.

1. Put on spacesuit and pack equipment.
2. Examine shuttle and make sure everything works.
3. Fly to Zennox.
4. Collect rock samples.
5. Return to ship.

Alex smiled and started the engine. Then the shuttle blasted off. Alex looked out the window and watched as Earth grew smaller and smaller.

Travel to Zennox took three months. Alex exercised every day. He wanted to be strong when he reached the distant planet. At last he arrived.

Present Tense	Past Tense	
happens	climbed	grew
put	felt	took
pack	asked	exercised
examine	read	wanted
make	smiled	reached
works	started	arrived
fly	blasted	
collect	looked	
return	watched	

Page 122

Answers will vary.

Page 124

1. He watched a scary movie about vampires.
2. Answers will vary but should include some of the following:
   Bats can fly.
   Vampire bats are small.
   They live in Central and South America.
   They drink blood.
   They have razor-sharp teeth.
   They usually don't bite humans.
   They can carry rabies and other diseases.
   They sleep during the day and eat at night.
   They don't suck blood; they lap it up.
   Their saliva keeps blood from clotting.
3. Wild animals can carry diseases.
4. Answers will vary but could include:
   Call 911.
   Tell parents.
   Go to a doctor.

Answers will vary.

Page 125

1. a
2. i
3. e
4. i
5. o
6. e
7. a
8. o
9. e
10. u
11. o
12. i
13. u
14. a

long a	long e	long i
ey	ea	i–e
ay	ee	igh
ai	ie	y

long o	long u
o	u–e
ough	u
oa	

1. e
2. i
3. e
4. e
5. i
6. i

one-syllable words: i
two-syllable words: e

Page 126

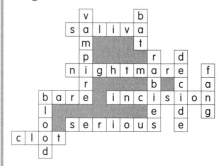

Page 127

1. true
2. false
3. true
4. false
5. true
6. true
7. false
8. true
9. false

Drawings will vary.

Read and Understand with Leveled Texts, Grade 3 • EMC 3443 • © Evan-Moor Corp.

Page 128

Answers will vary but could include:

birds only
lay eggs
eat seeds and insects
are covered with feathers

both birds and vampire bats
have wings
can fly
take care of their babies

vampire bats only
are covered with fur
are born live
feed babies milk from
  the mother's body

Page 130

1. His mother, who was a slave, was stolen from Moses and Susan Carver when George was a baby.
2. At seven, George knew so much about plants that he was called "the plant doctor."
   At ten, George left home to find a school he could go to.
3. Thomas Edison wanted George to work in his laboratory, but George wanted to teach.
4. He developed hundreds of ways to use peanuts and sweet potatoes so the farmers could grow things besides cotton and make the soil rich again.
5. He was the head of the agriculture program.
6. He got his nickname because of all his inventions made from peanuts and sweet potatoes.

Answers will vary.

Page 131

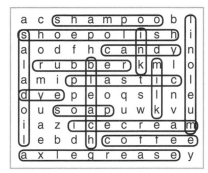

Page 132

ow	o
allow	below
brow	flow
crowd	own
flower	tow
town	

ran	grew
kept	found
began	blew

1. ran
2. kept
3. began
4. grew
5. found
6. blew

Page 133

Answers on lists will vary.

```
a c s h a m p o o b l
s h o e p o l i s h i
a o d f h c a n d y n
l r u b b e r k m l o
a m i p l a s t i c l
d y e p e o q s l n e
o u s o a p u w k v u
i a z i c e c r e a m
l e b d h c o f f e e
a x l e g r e a s e y
```

Underlined products will vary.

Page 134

Answers will vary but should reflect information in the story.

Page 136

1. A tornado is a powerful storm.
2. It is shaped like a thick funnel.
3. twister, cyclone
4. The low air pressure inside the funnel sucks things up like a vacuum cleaner.
5. Answers will vary but should include some of the following points:
   Trees can be pulled up by their roots.
   Cars can be turned over.
   Houses can explode.
   Roofs can be torn off buildings.
6. Stay away from windows.
   Go to a storm cellar.
   Listen to a battery radio.

Answers will vary.
 Example:
  People help each other clean up the mess, take care of people with injuries, and try to rebuild their homes and businesses.

Page 137

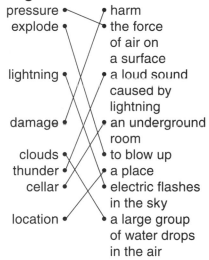

pressure • • harm
explode • • the force of air on a surface
lightning • • a loud sound caused by lightning
damage • • an underground room
clouds • • to blow up
thunder • • a place
cellar • • electric flashes in the sky
location • • a large group of water drops in the air

vacuum cleaner   lightning

Drawings will vary.

Page 138

1. call
2. fought
3. hollow
4. saw
5. ball / wall
6. caw

1. tornado
2. light
3. touch
4. dry
5. pass
6. scare
7. fly
8. explode
9. hurry
10. rise

Page 139

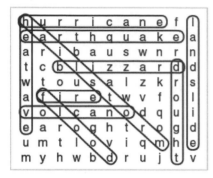

Answers will vary.

Page 140

1. You need four materials.
2. You add 1/4 cup of liquid detergent and one or more small objects.
3. A tornado-like funnel appears.
4. The small objects will look like things picked up by the funnel.

Page 142

1. Wording will vary but morals should contain the following ideas:

   Don't let yourself be distracted from your goal or purpose.

   If you move steadily toward your goal, you will succeed.

2. The wolf, the snake, and the bear learned the lesson. They were fooled into fighting with each other, and the old woman escaped.

   The hare learned the lesson. He lost the race because he stopped to take a nap instead of going on until he reached the finish line.

3. The old woman taught the lesson. She got the animals to focus on each other instead of on her so she could run away.

   The tortoise taught the lesson. By moving steadily toward his goal, he won the race.

4. Answers will vary.

Page 143

1. to be responsible

2. Herbert learned the lesson. He cleaned his room and said that he would never let it get that messy again.

3. *The Messiest Room in Town* There's no such thing as a dust monster.

4. **happy:** Herbert cleaned his room, so the dust monster went away, and Herbert surprised his family.

   not happy: Kim had to stay inside on a sunny Saturday to finish the homework she hadn't done during the week.

5. Answers will vary.

Page 144

1. They both tell how animals grow. They are both nonfiction.

2. **Grasshopper:** molts, hatches from an egg
   Koala: born live, tiny as a lima bean
   Both: needs food, does not look like an adult

3. *A Grasshopper's Life Cycle*

4. Answers will vary.

Page 145

1. the fisherman's wife
   She wanted to rule the sun and the moon.

   Icarus
   He wanted to fly higher and higher.

2. The enchanted fish that the fisherman caught came from the sea.

   Icarus fell into the sea and drowned when his wings melted.

3. **gives instructions:** Daedalus, fisherman's wife, fish
   always follows instructions: fisherman
   does not always follow instructions: Icarus, fish

4. Answers will vary.

Page 146

1. *George Washington Carver*
   When Granny Met Johnny Appleseed
   When Granny Met Johnny Appleseed
   George Washington Carver

2. **worked in the South:** Carver
   traveled west: Appleseed
   helped people grow plants for food: both
   was called "the plant doctor": Carver
   loved to grow things: both

3. *George Washington Carver*
   The story contains many facts about his life.

Get daily reading comprehension practice into your curriculum!

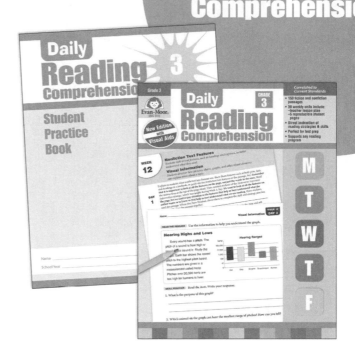

Daily Reading Comprehension

Supplement your reading instruction and prepare students for state testing with 150 daily lessons. In just 10 to 15 minutes a day, *Daily Reading Comprehension* presents students with the reading strategies and skills they need to become successful lifetime readers! 208 pages. *Correlated to current standards.*

You'll love *Daily Reading Comprehension* because it...

- *includes 150 original fiction and nonfiction passages accompanied by follow-up comprehension activities*

- *includes teacher pages with suggestions and ideas for guiding students through each passage*

- *provides instruction and practice on six reading strategies, such as asking questions and determining importance, and 12 important skills, such as cause and effect and nonfiction text features.*

ENHANCED
e-BOOK
available online
go to evan-moor.com

DAILY READING COMPREHENSION			
Grade Level	Teacher's Reproducible Edition	Student Pack (5 Student Books)	Class Pack (20 Student Books + Teacher's Edition)
1	EMC 3611	EMC 6371	EMC 9301
2	EMC 3612	EMC 6372	EMC 9302
3	EMC 3613	EMC 6373	EMC 9303
4	EMC 3614	EMC 6374	EMC 9304
5	EMC 3615	EMC 6375	EMC 9305
6	EMC 3616	EMC 6376	EMC 9306
7	EMC 3617	EMC 6377	EMC 9307
8	EMC 3618	EMC 6378	EMC 9308

Differentiate your class's reading instruction!

Nonfiction Reading Practice

Support the varied reading levels in your classroom! Every unit includes a reading selection at three reading levels and follow-up reading and writing activities to build comprehension. To further support students, each unit includes visual aids, Words to Know lists, comprehension questions (at three levels), graphic organizers, and writing forms. 208 pages. **Correlated to current standards.**

Each book gives you everything you need!

- *17 nonfiction reading units with selections at three different reading levels*
- *A reproducible test page to assess comprehension and vocabulary*
- *A vocabulary list for each unit*

Teacher pages
Introduce the topic and each article's vocabulary words.

Articles at 3 reading levels
Progress in difficulty from easiest to hardest.

Multiple-choice and constructed response questions
Assess students' vocabulary and comprehension.

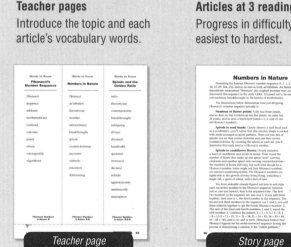

Teacher page

Story page

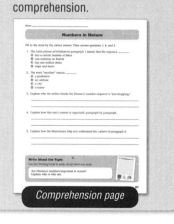

Comprehension page

Grade 1	EMC 3231
Grade 2	EMC 3232
Grade 3	EMC 3233
Grade 4	EMC 3234
Grade 5	EMC 3235
Grade 6	EMC 3236

Leveled Readers' Theater

Develop your students' fluency, automaticity, and comprehension with the meaningful reading practice in *Leveled Readers' Theater!* Each play contains parts for students reading below, on, or above grade level, so you can support all the students in your classroom! 160 pages. **Correlated to current standards.**

- *leveled plays accessible to students at all reading levels*
- *reproducible student scripts*
- *teaching guidelines with ideas for building background*
- *dictionary pages to introduce vocabulary*
- *follow-up activities that boost comprehension*

Grade 1	**Grade 3**	**Grade 5**
EMC 3481	EMC 3483	EMC 3485
Grade 2	**Grade 4**	**Grade 6**
EMC 3482	EMC 3484	EMC 3486